Enhanced Humans

■ ■ ■

Mystery Matrix

By Prince Handley

University of Excellence Press

UNIVERSITY OF EXCELLENCE PRESS
San Diego   London   Tel Aviv

ISBN-13: 978-0692435793
ISBN-10: 0692435794

Printed in the USA

The only Mystery Matrix book you need!

TABLE OF CONTENTS

FOREWORD

We are at the threshold of **the most cataclysmic— the worst and most evil—change in society** that Planet Earth has ever known.

This change is at the same time malevolent and opaque. You will NOT see through it—**unless you read this book**.

I am NOT talking about the New World Order—Global Governance—although that's a small part of it. I'm talking about **something so sinister—and at the same time—so appealing to every thinking person**.

I am talking about something that has its "core association" in age-old Biblical history, but—*at this moment*—is on the cutting edge of science and technology.

Do not be mistaken! Even though the triad of **government, military and education is spending millions of dollars in R & D**—with the financial support of banks and corporations—there is an unseen, dark force behind the "push" forward.

But … here is something even more amazing! There is also *currently* a hidden geopolitical "behind–the-scenes" amalgamation—a spiritual collusion—both human and other-worldly that is being orchestrated to facilitate **control** … of YOU and your family.

4

Don't worry about being left behind at the appearing of Messiah—that is, IF you KNOW Him. What you need to worry about NOW is:

■ Being left behind by enhanced humans.

■ Being tempted to sacrifice your autonomy.

■ Being "setup" to lose your children's DNA.

■ Being handed over to the Global Citizenry.

Thinking it's not possible? Then ... **you NEED this book. It will show you:**

■ The interconnection of the mystery matrix.

■ The players and their assignments.

■ The matrix relates to Israel and End Times.

■ The defined role of ISIS and Islamic terrorism.

■ Secret intel and prophecy for YOUR victory

■ Danger of NEW AI & 4th Industrial Revolution

Hang on! You're about to learn **WHAT is really happening, WHO is behind it and HOW to arrive on the other side victorious!**

Enhanced Humans

■ ■ ■

Mystery Matrix

GRIN AND BEAR IT

You are reading this book **while a new species of humans is being developed**. A super-human—enhanced human—with super intellect and physical abilities. This is the Ninth Edition published in 2025.

This book is a real—non-fiction—presentation: true, accurate and contemporary. Current—plus already planned—research associated with real documented "enhanced human" developments are discussed.

This section, *GRIN and Bear It*, is just that: **it's too late … it's already happening**. What you are going to learn about is real, it is contemporary and it is catastrophic. **You will have to "bear it."** However, how you do so will determine your destiny: in this life … and forever.

As for the **GRIN**, you will learn about:

   ■ **G**enetic alteration or modification.

   ■ **R**obotics

   ■ **I**nformation technology

   ■ **N**anotechnology

GRIN technology via the use of AI is being used successfully in retailing and **HR recruiting**. [79]. These will be discussed separately, but for now let's take a test ride. See if you're up to the rest of this book. **Warning – you haven't seen anything yet**. We're just scratching the surface here at the start. [In the section below we will discuss NBIC and more advanced items.

Computer scientist Bill Joy, and many other writers, have identified cluster groups of technological advances that

7

they esteem critical to the future of humanity. Joy warns that these advances have potential to be used by "elites" for either good or evil.[1]

For example, when super humans become advanced— *enhanced*—to a stage where the ordinary *normal* human is no longer relevant other than for "slave" activities, then ... genocide—*mass destruction*—of the normal humans will become efficient in terms of Global Governance. (More about this later ... hang on!)

Joy and other writers feel that such techno-human advances could be used as "good shepherds" for the rest of humanity ... OR ... decide everyone else—the normal *original* human—is superfluous and push for mass extinction of those made unnecessary by technology.

AI could become 'capable of manipulating or deceiving humans,' [92] Artificial intelligence could gain the upper hand over humanity and pose "catastrophic" risks under the Darwinian rules of evolution, a new report April 2023 warns.

"Evolution by natural selection could give rise to "selfish behavior" in AI as it strives to survive," author and AI researcher Dan Hendrycks argues in the new paper *"Natural Selection Favors AIs over Humans."*

"We argue that natural selection creates incentives for AI agents to act against human interests. Our argument

relies on two observations," Hendrycks, the director of the Center for AI Safety, said in the report. *"Firstly, natural selection may be a dominant force in AI development... Secondly, evolution by natural selection tends to give rise to selfish behavior."* [93]

The report comes as tech experts and leaders across the world sound the alarm on how quickly artificial intelligence is expanding in power without what they argue are adequate safeguards.

Rep. Lance Gooden, R-Texas, says that Americans could *"get to the point where someday we're all very afraid"* of artificial intelligence after more than a thousand business leaders penned an open letter in 2023 urging new AI developments to be put on pause for six months.

"This is something that is going to sneak up on us, and we'll get to the point where we're in too deep to really make meaningful changes before it's too late," Gooden tells Fox News Digital.

In November 2022, Microsoft unveiled ChatGPT, an AI-powered chatbot that engages in human-like dialogue and can generate responses, analyze data and text — potentially threatening careers in a wide range of industries, from customer service, tech and media jobs.

But, let's look at some more positive and recent results of ChatGPT from interactions with highly trained human professionals.

9

LETS LOOK AT SOME GOOD CHATGPT RESULTS

Study finds ChatGPT's latest bot behaves like humans, only better!

A study in 2024 revealed that the most recent version of the chatbot, version 4, was not distinguishable from its human counterparts. In instances **when the bot chose less common human behaviors, it was more cooperative and altruistic.** [110]

AI Chatbots Defeated Doctors at Diagnosing Illness!

In a 2024 study Dr. Adam Rodman—an expert in internal medicine at Beth Israel Deaconess Medical Center in Boston—helped design, **doctors who were given ChatGPT-4 along with conventional resources did only slightly better than doctors who did not have access to the bot.** And, **to the researchers' surprise, ChatGPT alone outperformed the doctors.** [111]

SO WHY ARE HUMANS SKEPTICAL OF CHATGPT

"I am worried about being pulled over and questioned by a robot someday. I don't want to live in a society where a task of government that should be fulfilled by real life people are being replaced with AI," said Lance Gooden, who we mentioned previously. *"That's very scary to me, and I think we need to be very cautious."* [96]

Concerning privacy and data collection, many are beginning to feel that AI can lead to discrimination [we will cover this later] and push for software engineers (and algorithm designers) to study Human Rights laws.[54] But before we go into an in-depth discussion of GRIN, **let's look at ONE of the most intrusive and feared uses of AI today: surveillance of the individual.**

SURVEILLANCE OF THE INDIVIDUAL

First, we will scope **the usage of surveillance without discussing the inclusion or need for AI.** Veripol (developed by experts at Cardiff University) uses a combination of automatic **text analysis and artificial intelligence to recognize when somebody has been lying or exaggerating to the police.**

Using algorithms the machine can carefully analyze various features in the text, such as adjectives, acronyms, verbs, nouns, punctuation marks and numbers.[68]

China's social rating system, which was announced by the ruling Communist Party in 2014, has become "modus operandi" for many in China already. Some already—at this time—are required to have a **minimum number of (walking) steps on their Fitbit in order to "sign in" to their social media accounts.**

It the People's Republic of China's plan continues, every footstep, keystroke, like, dislike, social media contact, and posting tracked by the state will affect one's social rating.[58]

A plan released just recently by the Beijing municipal government dictates that personal **creditworthiness points will be used to reward and/or punish individuals**—and companies—**by granting or denying them access to public services like healthcare, travel, and employment.** High scoring "Green Channel" people can more easily access social opportunities. Those who actions are disapproved of by the state will be restricted ...**even to having passports revoked.**

You are probably already familiar with AI "facial recognition" cameras in China's traffic areas used to identify people who jaywalk or disobey the "OK to walk" lights. **Some have even lost passports due to multiple violations.**

How would YOU like ever present cameras that can track your identity and locations? **While the answer is likely to be "No" for many in Israel and the West, the scenario is becoming a reality in China.**

Large internet companies are yielding **great revenue implementing "AI" advances to help with Beijing's surveillance** of its citizens—and companies.[59]

Now that we have discussed the minimally invasive—but probably one of the most concerning—areas of AI, we will continue with GRIN.

GENETIC ALTERATION OR MODIFICATION

Eugenics is the science and practice of selective human breeding. In the late 1800's eugenics came into being for the "so-called" purpose of improving the quality of humanity. This was to be implemented by discouraging reproduction by persons having genetic defects or inheritable undesirable traits—and encouraging reproduction by persons presumed to have inheritable desirable traits.

This theory became popular in the early 20th Century, but is no longer *outwardly* taken seriously due to the horrific practices of "racial hygiene" experiments by the Nazis in Germany.

However, there is a NEW form of eugenics—not only being espoused but heavily financed in research— to create super-humans via genetic modification of human genes in eggs, sperm and early-stage embryos.

Human genetic modification (or "gene editing") can be used in two very different ways. **Somatic genome editing** changes the genes in a patient's cells to treat a medical condition. A few gene therapies are approaching clinical use but remain extraordinarily expensive.

By contrast, **heritable genome editing would change genes in eggs, sperm, or early embryos to try to control the traits of a future child.** Such alterations would affect every cell of the resulting person **and all subsequent generations.**

Because of the modification of the cell structure in the embryo, subsequent generations will inherit these modifications. And ... **with NO re-setting the process**.

This NEW form is known as **genetic engineering.** Genetic engineering is a biotechnological application where the DNA or genes of organisms are manipulated according to the requirement.

You probably are wondering right now if what you are reading is mere conjecture. Well ... read this report from the US government sponsored by the National Science Foundation and the US Department of Commerce: *Converging Technologies for Improving Human Performance.*[2] This report includes such items as "brain-machine" interfacing (BMI), which we will cover later in this book.

Also, the acronym **NBIC** was introduced into public discourse via this report in 2014 for **N**anotechnology, **B**iotechnology, **I**nformation **t**echnology and **C**ognitive **s**cience as the most popular term for emerging and converging technologies.

With CRISPR-Cas9 technology, humans can now rapidly change the evolutionary course of animals or plants by inserting genes that can easily spread through entire populations. Evolutionary geneticist Asher Cutter proposes that we call this evolutionary meddling "genetic welding" and that *"we [should] think about genes having a 50:50 chance of getting passed from parent to offspring, but this isn't always the case. In a natural phenomenon known as "genetic drive," some genes are able to bias their own transmission so that they are much more likely to be inherited."* [88]

WARNING ~ Genetic welding is the human-mediated version of this: introducing genes that have an unfair advantage when it comes to heritability into natural populations.

In mid-March 2023 the Third International Summit on Human Genome put out its closing statement. *"Heritable human genome editing—editing embryos that are then implanted to establish a pregnancy, which can pass on their edited DNA—"remains unacceptable at this time,"* the committee concluded.

"Public discussions and policy debates continue and are important for resolving whether this technology should be used." The message was loud and clear: **Scientists don't yet know how to safely edit embryos**." [89]

Human enhancement, or "germ-line engineering," involves making "improvements" in reproductive cells.

15

These changes will be passed on to subsequent generations. This presents valid bioethics and moral questions:

Will criminal—*underground elements*—develop and market enhanced-human embryos?

When enhanced-humans become dominant in numbers, influence or power, what happens to the normal—non-enhanced—humans?

Will they become victims of genocide … or will they be mere slaves or servants: an "inferior" breed?"

Will enhanced humans automatically receive the *Mark of the Beast*?

**SEE THE SECTION ON
TECHNOLOGICAL SINGULARITY
FOR A COMPETITIVE MODE
OF HUMAN ENHANCEMENT**

● ROBOTICS

Robots are used in security, medicine, industry and military—and now starting to be used in personal areas of service. As robotics, autonomous vehicles and drones become more widely used across cities, pollution and traffic congestion may reduce, making towns and cities more pleasant places to spend time outside.

But the researchers also warned that advances in robotics and automation could be damaging to the environment.

For instance, robots and drones might generate new sources of waste and pollution themselves, with potentially substantial negative implications for urban nature. Cities might have to be re-planned to provide enough room for robots and drones to operate, potentially leading to a loss of green space. And they could also increase existing social inequalities, such as unequal access to green space.[70]

Robotics is a combination of branches of mechanical engineering, electrical engineering and computer science that deals with the design, construction, operation, and application of robots, as well as computer systems for their control, sensory feedback, and information processing.

These technologies deal with automated machines that can take the place of humans in dangerous environments or manufacturing processes, or resemble humans in appearance, behavior, and/or cognition. Many of today's robots are inspired by nature contributing to the field of bio-inspired robotics.[10]

As the pandemic wore on humanoid robots that could perform general tasks became increasingly important. They could move heavy objects in warehouses, assist with last-yard deliveries, and potentially be involved in other tasks **where low human-to-human contact was preferable** for safety reasons.

However, imagine you're at my house. I get firewood delivered once a year. I could not possibly use a [firewood-stacking] robot 24/7. And so something that can do firewood loading and unloading in my woodshed once a year, **and then infill other tasks as the duty cycle demands**, is more useful."

Before the pandemic, if a customer needed some assistance getting a robot up and running, an engineer could just hop on a plane and be on site in a few hours; but that was NOT an option in those days. That forced Agility Robotics to push for product maturity, enabling **out-of-the-box deployment**, with more urgency.[72]

The ideal AI robot would be a replication of the human thought process: a man-made robot with human intellectual abilities. This would include the ability to learn just about anything, the ability to reason, the ability to use language and the ability to formulate original ideas.

The **AI robot** gathers facts about a situation through sensors or human input. The computer compares this information to stored data and decides what the information signifies. The computer runs through various possible actions and predicts which action will be most successful based on the collected information. However, **the robot can only solve problems that it is programmed to solve; it has no—at this juncture—innate analytical ability … at least not YET!**

However, **Micro-Robots in your veins are in the making.** Scientists have created an army of microscopic four-legged robots too small to seen with the naked eye that walk when stimulated by a laser and could be injected into the body through hypodermic needles. These micro-robots could clean arteries, stimulate heartbeats, and regulate blood pressure.[73]

WHAT ABOUT WHEN ROBOTS ARE CONFUSED

Robots are confused when uncertainty arises. The inability to generalize or adapt with changing conditions is a big problem. **The prime goal at this point is how humans learn, think, plan and implement.** If robots can simulate emotion, they can save memory and processing time. Marvin Minsky shows how emotion could be used to build better robots and artificial intelligence in his book: *The Society of Mind* and *The Emotion Machine.*[12]

BUT A ROBOT CONDUCTED PRECISE SURGERY

Robot that watched surgery videos performs with skill of human doctor.

Breakthrough training system opens 'new frontier' in medical robotics.

A robot, trained for the first time by watching videos of seasoned surgeons, executed the same surgical procedures as skillfully as the human doctors, say researchers.

The successful use of **imitation learning** to train surgical robots **eliminates the need to program robots with each individual move required during a medical procedure** and brings the field of robotic surgery closer to true autonomy, **where robots could perform complex surgeries without human help.**

"It's really magical to have this model and all we do is feed it camera input and it can predict the robotic movements needed for surgery," said senior author Axel Krieger. *"We believe this marks a significant step forward toward a new frontier in medical robotics."* [106]

ROBOTS AND THE DEVELOPMENT OF CYBORGS

A number of robotics experts predict that robotic evolution will ultimately turn us into cyborgs— humans integrated with machines. Conceivably, people in the future could load their minds into a sturdy robot and live for thousands of years.[11]

Futurist Ian Pearson says, *"The robot is really just a front end for some smartness to exist somewhere—like the cloud—on the network."*[16]

Actually, today there are many people who have voluntarily become cyborgs: there are seven (7) real-life human cyborgs.[13]

There is another scenario, however, that is more scientifically and scripturally feasible. And that involves actual—present day—cyborgs. I am talking about **human brain–machine interface.** We will cover this in a later section of this book, but basically it involves **connectivity of the human brain with external software or information.** Instead of robots receiving intel from humans, the converse is affected: **the human brain receives input from external—connected— information.** This is REAL, absolutely credible, and opens up myriads of spiritual, moral and ethical dementias.

The human population worldwide is growing at a rate of 2% a year; while the robot population worldwide is growing at a rate of 30% a year.[14] Ian Pearson predicted that the robot population would be higher than humans in developed countries by 2025.[15] Doesn't look like it yet.

March 27, 2015, there was an announcement on major news media that surgical robots were now being used in certain critical operations because they were more accurate than human surgeons. We have verified this in previous sections of this book. **Following are listed some of the benefits of surgical robots.**

Robotic surgical methods have certain advantages over traditional, open surgical methods, including:

- Enhanced dexterity for minute procedures

- Expanded range of motion

- Improved three-dimensional imaging of the surgical site

- Stabilization, which removes any instability inherent in human hands

- Virtual training capacity

- Less pain and trauma to the patient

- Shorter recovery times with fewer complications [21]

Robots also have the potential of improving quantity, quality and quintessential efficiency—especially when combined with artificial Intelligence (AI)—in the following ways:

■ Productivity in the marketplace.

■ Enhanced human brain-machine interfacing controlling satellite robotics which "thinks" purchase and sells with programmed marketing.

■ Optimum creativity is made possible by interfacing of supply-demand chains with decision making.

■ Reverse engineering with cyber-brain decisions and implementation based upon optimal pathways.

■ Stronger, healthier, more adaptive and self-healing "super" humans.

Regardless of some concern about AI underpinning dangerous foundations, humanoid robots can have a valuable position in the performance of more dangerous—or mundane—tasks.

Akinsoft established a factory in Turkey in December 2017 (Akin Robotics Factory) to manufacture robots that can process input from hearing, smelling and speaking … **plus, they can use the internet**.

Sophia, the world's first AI-powered humanoid has nice-looking features; she manifests kindness, wisdom, and compassion; along with a sense of humor. She holds eye contact and can express emotions while recognizing faces and understanding human speech.

The Japanese government has started funding **"elder care" robots** to help supply the shortage of healthcare workers. There are 20 different types of robots caring for clients in Tokyo's Shintomi nursing home.[55]

Another use of robots is in the "micro" world where they can be used for **search-and-rescue operations** ... or for **inspection of hazardous environments** ... or **for spy operations**. Cybugs with micro-backpacks for drones have been used for many years already. Some scientists have created UAVs (Unmanned aerial Vehicles) smaller than 6 inches—**but 6 inches is mini, not micro. Insects are micro**.

In 2023 MIT researchers developed a robotic hand that uses high-resolution touch sensing to accurately identify an object after grasping it just one time.

Many robotic hands pack all their powerful sensors into the fingertips, so an object must be in full contact with those fingertips to be identified, which can take multiple grasps. Other designs use lower-resolution sensors spread along the entire finger, but these don't capture as much detail, so multiple regrasps are often required.

Instead, the MIT team built a robotic finger with a rigid skeleton encased in a soft outer layer that has multiple high-resolution sensors incorporated under its transparent "skin." [90]

NOTE: One economic downside of robotics is that **robots are on track to wipe out almost a tenth of the world's manufacturing jobs** (20 million positions) with the brunt borne by lower-income areas in developed nations by 2030, Oxford Economics says.[67]

DARPA (Defense Advanced Research Projects Agency) has a "hybrid" (HI-MEMS) project as part of its cyborg program to create a stable tissue-machine interface. Researchers envision **tiny backpacks for these cybugs that are filled with miniaturized pressure, temperature and chemical detection sensors as well as communications, microphones and cameras.**[56]

Controlling the movement—steering them—may have several options, such as: electromechanical and neural stimulation; optical cues with micro-optical visual presentation; and direct electrical muscle stimulation.

DARPA is planning a "bug sized" robot Olympics style competition to **test and compare strength, speed and agility** for its new SHRIMP program (Short-range Independent Microrobotic Platforms).[57]

Later in the book we will discuss the Mystery Matrix. However, at this juncture it will be advantageous to discuss just HOW robotics can and may be used to serve the **New Global Governance.** [22] Here are some ways in which robotics may serve the Evil Empire:

- Image of the Beast

- Monitoring public places and individual houses and businesses (robots would be assigned to specific addresses with legal warrants).

- Security – NOT your security, but the government's.

- Housing "shell" for AI of the Anti-Christ demonic system to carry out orders. i.e., Robots may be used to perform orders programmed into them.

INFORMATION TECHNOLOGY

All the cloud's a stage. IT transformation will continue to get star billing this year, and **the main players were evident heading into 2025.** The cloud set the stage where digital transformation started to play out. In the world of "everything as a service," efficient use of cloud resources is a pre-requisite to good performances from the rest of the 4th Industrial Revolution cast. AI, 5G, blockchain, process automation, autonomous devices (robots, drones and vehicles), and virtual (aka augmented or extended) reality will take up the most important roles.[71]

Human brains age. **Some believe that a computer brain would provide a physical system that could maintain itself indefinitely.** In Dan Simmons' *Hyperion* series, Future Human Society is under the coordination of a collective of advanced AI's that monitor the technological workings of the vast human galactic civilization.[17]

Artificial intelligence (AI) is the branch of computer science that deals with the simulation of human intelligence and behavior in computers. However, this brings to light a reflection concerning **"brain tampering and AI"** as to *"What it means to be human?"*

In 2012, it was the night before Christmas ... and all through MIT laboratory on Vassar street in Cambridge some mice were stirring. More than two years of "long shot" research effort supported an extraordinary hypothesis. *"Not only was it possible to identify brain cells involved in the encoding of a single memory, but those specific cells could be manipulated to create a whole new 'memory' of an event that never happened."*

The long-term goal of nanotechnology is to be able to fully manipulate molecular and atomic structures. Since humans are made of the same basic building blocks as the natural world, **nanotechnology will probably enable the ability to change human tissues and cells at the molecular level.**

As tech trends such as Artificial Intelligence (**AI**) and Robotic Process Automation (**RPA**) become more pervasive, the world will look to brands who can deliver with accuracy and real-time efficiency. **Digital twins are very useful for helping us to predict outcomes and measure performance.** Advancements such as genome mapping and gene therapy could become more viable in the future. **Digital twin technology could finally eliminate the need for clinical trials in humans** as we work to manage future medical challenges. [91]

This brings to the surface another question: *"If memories can be manipulated at will, what does it mean to have a past? **If we can erase a bad memory, or create a good one, how do we create a true sense of self?**"*[26] Julian Barnes, in his memoir *Nothing to be Frightened Of*, writes, ***"Memory is identity.*** *You are what you have done; what you have done is in your memory; what you remember defines who you are."* [27]

While we are discussing brain manipulation, memory, AI and *"What it means to be human,"* controversial Italian neurosurgeon Sergio Canavero claimed he could perform the world's first ever human **head** transplant in 2017, despite ethical and scientific reservations from many of his colleagues.

And in 2017 Canavero announced at a press conference in Vienna on Friday that a surgical team led by his collaborator in China, Xiaoping Ren, had "successfully" transferred a head from one human cadaver to another.

There are ethical problems from several considerations (*religious being one*) to the simple 'ickiness-factor' which are also likely to slow down the progress of such a development.

"In this case, you're not altering the cortex," said Patricia Scripko, a neurologist and bioethicist at the Salinas Valley Memorial Healthcare System in California, who does not believe the procedure is possible, but insists it is not objectionable.[8]

Check this out: Researchers from the Royal Melbourne Institute of Technology (RMIT) have created the world's first electronic multi-state memory cell which **mirrors the brain's ability to simultaneously process and store multiple strands of information.**

The device which is 10,000 times thinner than a human hair is a ***"vital step towards creating a bionic brain,"*** the scientists said. The new nano cell can store information in multiple states because it is analogue. Dr

Hussein Nili, researcher, says, *"While these new devices are able to store much more information than conventional digital memories (which store just 0s and*

1s), it is their brain-like ability to **remember and retain previous information** *that is exciting."*[7]

The purpose of AI is to posture—copy and transfer—human thinking into non-human systems. As synergy grows between health, medicine and biotechnology, the next logical phase will be to—*further*—champion human brain–machine interfacing (BMI): to augment our own intellectual powers with the results of our technology.

Raymond Kurzweil says: ***"We'll have very powerful little computers that can travel through our bloodstream,*** *that will be the size of blood cells and they'll actually communicate wirelessly with our neurons, so we'll be actually able to enhance our own thinking capacity, speed up our thinking, increase human memory, increase our cognitive abilities and pattern recognition* **by combining our biological intelligence with these new forms of non-biological intelligence."**

If you read the above statement closely, you will see that **we are closing in on our next topic: Nanotechnology.** Stick around … I'm going to explain where we're going with all this. **You are going to receive revelation knowledge before this is all over.**

You will know more than 99.9% of the populace—and **you will be able to detect the *Mystery Matrix* as it is evolving NOW … and in the future!**

30

NANOTECHNOLOGY

Nanotech describes technologies developed to perform complex tasks at the scale of molecules or atoms. For relevance, **one nanometer in diameter is about 100,000 times smaller than the width of a human hair**. Biotech goals—aimed at medicine and human health—are looking to viruses for creative ideas, because viruses insert their own genes into human cells to replicate themselves.

The idea is to deliver healthy genes to target cells and repair errors or malfunctions in DNA that cause disease. Also,one goal is to utilize targeted gene therapy with nanoparticles to stop—or destroy—cancer formations.

Using **nanotechnology**, biotechnology, human brain-machine interfacing and other specialties addressed in this book, **transhumanists** strive—are actively involved—in creating the ultimate human. The chief goal is life extension and biological improvement. However, enhancement versus "other" modifications can leave a wide spectrum of uncertainty.

"Transhuman" literally means *beyond human*. Transhumanists consist of life extensionists, techno-optimists, Singularitarians, biohackers, roboticists, "AI" proponents, and futurists who embrace radical science and technology to improve the human condition. The **most important aim for many transhumanists is to**

overcome human mortality, a goal some believe is achievable by 2045.[20]

Nanotechnology potentially provides the ability to order and change molecular and atomic structures. The same basic building blocks are present in humans as are in the natural world, thus enabling nanotechnology to change human tissues and cells at the molecular level.

Better IQ, appearance, and capabilities are key aims of human enhancement. "These enhancements will undoubtedly benefit many, but they also bring up important moral, ethical, and legal questions.

Some worry that human enhancements **may create undesirable pressures to enhance**. Would it be possible to compete for a job if everyone else was enhanced mentally, to compete in athletics if everyone else was strength-enhanced, or compete for a spouse if you were not physically enhanced? These are legitimate concerns, but they are probably not strong enough to prevent, or even slow, enhancement technologies."[29]

People involved in the creative fields would have expanded access to creative streams of thought and implementation. Not only productivity—in factories and personal endeavors—but recreation and sports will also be augmented. And, also, in the military.

The electric vehicle market has been experiencing explosive growth, with global sales surpassing $1 trillion (approx. KRW 1,283 trillion) in 2022 and domestic sales exceeding 108,000 units. Inevitably, **demand is growing for high-capacity batteries that can extend EV driving range**. Recently, a joint team of researchers from POSTECH and Sogang University developed a functional polymeric binder for stable, high-capacity anode material that could **increase the current EV range at least 10-fold.** [94]

A report revealed that scientists in Poland were working on liquid body armor technology that uses specially designed liquid to protect against bullets, according to Reuters. With STF (also known as ooblek), a bullet's force is absorbed by the liquid, and then dissipated outwards through the fluid. The US Army has also worked on such armor with the University of Delaware.

Nanotechnology can be—and is already being— used to produce changes *inside* the host's body. In the past, geneticists have used microbiological "vectors" to transfer animal and plant genes from one species into another. But now, **"vectors" are a new method of transferring—transporting—sub-atomic material**.

The "vectors" are essentially biological "trucks" that transport DNA building materials AND agents— *workers*—into human cell structure.

To change a human body—to repair, to enhance, or to fix a mistake—you need a "delivery system." Some of these delivery systems can be formulated to "time-release." The delivery system can be structured via virus or bacteria. A virus can be used like a "suitcase" where genetic mutation material is packed. And then … the goal is to target the specific cell(s). However, getting the payload **where** you want **when** you want it—is the nightmare **unless you have a map.**

Virtual Receptor Mapping (VRM) is the most exciting development in genetic engineering. Cellular tempo, muscle efficiency, oxygenation, neural regeneration, elasticity, sensory function and pain suppression are all fields of research and development … especially for the military.

In addition to the **National Nanotechnology Initiative** discussed previously, the USA has the **Center for Soldier Nanotechnologies** (CSN) which is working on **interfacing the human nervous system with electronic (machine) devices to develop a "Super Soldier" or "Cyborg Soldier."**

One nanometer is a billionth of a meter, or 10^{-9} of a meter. Here are a few illustrative examples:

■ There are 25,400,000 nanometers in an inch.
■ A sheet of newspaper is about 100,000 nanometers thick.
■ On a comparative scale, if a marble were a nanometer, then one meter would be the size of the Earth.[18]

The University of Texas announced what is called the **smallest and best nanomotor ever built**. Mechanical engineer Donglei Fan led a group of engineers who built **a motor 500 times smaller than a grain of salt**. Measuring 1 micrometer across, it **could fit inside a human cell**.[19] Note: A "micrometer" (old term, "micron") is one-millionth of a meter, or one 25-thousandth of an inch.

Let me summarize: a "vector" can be any vehicle that can carry—transport—genetic information and gain entry into a cell. And ... with genetic mapping ... **once inside the cell, the "workers" go about their respective jobs** of: **1.** Splicing human genes at predetermined locations ... OR ... **2.** Filing genetic information that can be—at any time—downloaded for production of NEW—hybrid—cells. **WARNING**: These cells are NOT just "enhanced" cells. **They will no longer be human.**

WARNING

These cells are NOT just enhanced.
They are no longer human cells!

Even If new hybrid cells are not produced, the very fact of **enhancement**—due to the influence of uncertainty, let's call it what it is: modification—**could easily have deleterious results. Here are just a few examples**:

■ Brain modification allowing receptors to gain access or receive messages from paranormal and Satanic occult sources.

■ Downloading via the transfer of artificial intelligence (AI) information through brain-machine interfacing, a **desire** for the "Mark of the Beast."

■ Corrupted spermatozoa which could fertilize an ovum producing a hybrid being: a non—*other than normal*—human life form.

■ Receiving fallen—demonically anointed—influence via psycho-neural pathways.

Cybernetics has been defined as the scientific study of **control—automatic control systems—and communication in the animal and the machine**. It basically concerns a "closed loop" with feedback as to what happens when change happens.

Automatic control systems—especially as regards to Artificial Intelligence (AI) via input to the human brain—Brain Machine Interfacing (BMI) and Nanotechnology will result in **internal programming that will substitute** for **Normal Human Nature** ... which is concomitant with Transhumanism (= beyond human).

The horizon of hope for nanotech providing advances in medicine, technology, metallurgy, commerce and sustainability is bright. However, substances get more reactive as their particles get smaller—the surface area is greater relative to the volume—providing a larger surface on which chemical reactions MAY occur for a given amount of the substance. **The size and shape of nanoparticles may affect their bioactivity and toxicity.**[60]

The ability of nanoparticles to interact with living systems increases because they can often penetrate the skin, enter the bloodstream via the lungs, and cross the blood-brain barrier. Once inside the body, there may be further biochemical reactions that pose danger, such as the creation of free radicals that damage cells and DNA.

We have discussed in part some future reflections of **both the benefits and possible dangers of nanotech**. But what are some specific time-projected risks that **may** be associated with nanotechnology—and **when** might we expect their arrival upon the scene? The **beneficial assets of nanotech** are seemingly limitless; however, just as many of the great advancements of the past, **there are risks** associated with its development and implementation. **Let's look at WHAT risks may be present on Planet Earth ... and WHEN to expect them.** [61]

NANOTECHNOLOGY RISKS

Real Risk: Nanopollutants
When: Now

Nanopollutants are nanoparticles small enough to enter your lungs or be absorbed by your skin. Nanopollutants can be natural or man-made. Nanoparticles are used in some of the products found on shelves today, like anti-aging cosmetics and sunscreen. The highest risk we have found is to the workers in nano-technology research and manufacturing processes.

Potential Risk: Privacy Invasion
When 1 to 10 years

Virtually undetectable surveillance devices could dramatically increase spying on governments, corporations and private citizens.

Potential Risk: Economic Upheaval
When: 5 to 20 years

Molecular manufacturing is the assembly of products one molecule at a time. It could make the same products you see today, but far more precisely and at a very low cost. It is unclear whether this would bring boom or bust to the global economy.

Potential Risk: Nanotech weapons
When: 5 to 10 years

Untraceable weapons made with nanotechnology could be smaller than an insect with the intelligence of a supercomputer. Resulting both in possible nanotech and biotech technology arms race.

So far, you can see HOW **nanotechnology**—with its precise sub-atomic accuracy and delivery—in conjunction with **biotech** and **artificial intelligence (AI)** can be used to enhance the human condition while at the same time approaching—possibly crossing—the point of no return, especially with regard to **Singularity**, **cyber-genetics**—and even—**robotics**.

Let's take some time to discuss **Technological Singularity**: WHAT it is, HOW it works, and WHY many in the scientific field believe it can overtake us. By "overtake' ... I mean "pass us and still look back." **You might want to go pray for a while before reading this!**

TECHNOLOGICAL SINGULARITY

At some point the various technological systems we have—as they keep progressing—will overtake us in intelligence ... and possibly—*hopefully*—discipline. They will eventually initiate the creation of hyper-intelligences where "machines" surpass human intelligences and continue the non-linear trend of creating even more hyper-intelligences. Eventually, humans are on the lower totem pole of the equation.

Technological singularity is the hypothesis that accelerating progress in technologies will cause a runaway effect wherein artificial intelligence will exceed human intellectual capacity and control, thus radically changing civilization in an event called the **singularity**.[3] Because the capabilities of such an intelligence may be impossible for a human to comprehend, the **technological singularity is an occurrence beyond which events may become unpredictable, unfavorable, or even unfathomable** [4]

ANALYSIS FROM 2015
We may reach singularity by 2040.

ANALYSIS FROM 2023
Humanity may reach singularity by 2030.

ANALYSIS FROM 2025
Ray Kurzweil, previously 2045, now 2032.

There are some in the scientific community who feel that Technological Singularity is NOT probable. However, many prominent voices from science and education disagree.

Professor Stephen Hawking (1942 -2018), Cambridge University physicist asserted that new developments in the field of Artificial Intelligence (AI) mean that within a few decades, **computers that are thousands of times more powerful than in existence today may decide to usurp their creators and effectively end humanity's multi-year dominance on earth**.

A translation company developed a metric, *Time to Edit (TTE)*, to calculate the time it takes for professional human editors to fix AI-generated translations compared to human ones. **This may help quantify the speed toward singularity.**

An AI that can translate speech as well as a human could change society. Language is one of the most difficult AI challenges, but a computer that could close that gap could theoretically show signs of Artificial General Intelligence (AGI). AGI is covered more specifically in the section below titled *AI and the 4th Industiral Revolution*.

AI entrepreneurs are also making estimates on when we will reach singularity and they are more optimistic than researchers. This is expected as they benefit from increased interest in AI:

Elon Musk expects development of an artificial intelligence **smarter than the smartest of humans by 2026** [103]

Demis Hassabis, founder of DeepMind: **2035** [104]

Ray Kurzweil, computer scientist, entrepreneur and writer of 5 national best sellers including *The Singularity Is Near*: **Previously 2045, in 2024: Now 2032**. [105]

REACHING AGI IS INEVITABLE TO MOST EXPERTS

Reaching AGI may seem like a wild prediction, but it seems like quite a reasonable goal when you consider these facts:

> Human intelligence is fixed unless we somehow merge our cognitive capabilities with machines. **Elon Musk's neural lace startup aims to do this** but research on brain-computer interfaces is in still promising but progressive stages.

> Machine intelligence depends on algorithms, processing power, and memory. Processing power and memory have been growing at an exponential rate. **As for algorithms, until now we have been good AI supplying machines with the necessary algorithms to use their processing power and memory effectively**.

Considering that our intelligence is fixed and machine intelligence is growing, it is only a matter of time before machines surpass us unless there's some hard limit to their intelligence. We haven't encountered such a limit yet.

This is a good analogy for understanding exponential growth. While machines can seem dumb right now, they can grow quite smart, quite soon.

ETHICAL PARAMETERS

There is a school of thought that if we "enhance" the brain to a level where one day we can have a symbiotic relationship with Singularity it may keep humanity from being "usurped."

There are several ethical "layers" of thought involved with technological singularity, particularly as it relates to **Brian Machine Interfacing (BMI)**. For example, BMI's could also make vulnerable groups (handicapped, queers, minorities, etc.) forsake their own values by medicalizing and 'fixing" them.[7]

The longest-term goal is transhumanism (we will cover this later in the book) … enabling the next step in the human race and overcoming our limitations (vis-à-vis being "usurped" by Singularity).by enhancing the processing power of our brains. Elon Musk believes that only by creating a high bandwidth BMI will we have a chance of keeping up with Singularity. The question: **How to retain what makes us human in the quest to become super-cyborgs?** [To be discussed later in the book.]

BMI technology is emerging as one of the hottest areas in the global startup investment community. Many companies believe that brain technology will eventually evolve into an entirely new form of communication where **users will be able to "think" words which will be converted into text without the need for speaking or writing.**

Elon Musk—PayPal, SpaceX and Tesla electric car genius—stated that, "with artificial intelligence, we are summoning the demon," and placing **AI as more of a potential threat to the annihilation of the human race than nuclear war**. However, read on …

Musk recently revealed that his **Neuralink** startup is close to announcing **the first brain-machine interface to connect human brains and computers**: an "ultra-high bandwidth" connection. He states that such an interface is essential to enhance the human brain if humans are to compete with technology in the future.[62]

Neuralink projected they would outfit human brains with faster input and output starting in 2020, based upon "thread" technology (threads can be implanted in human brains with less potential impact to surrounding brain tissue). **The long-term goal is to attain a type of "symbiosis with Artificial Intelligence."** [69] Neuralink plans to use a robot they have created that operates in process similar to a sewing machine to implant the thin threads (between 4 and 6 μm) **deep within brain tissue**

where they can implement "read and write" operations at high data volume.

BMI technology is emerging as one of the hottest areas in the global startup investment community. Many companies believe that brain technology will eventually evolve into an entirely new form of communication where **users will be able to "think" words which will be converted into text without the need for speaking or writing.**

Neuralink, the neurotechnology company founded by Elon Musk, was at first having **a rough initial go-round with the Food and Drug Administration's human-trials application process**. The company also faced additional investigations by two other U.S. government agencies. These setbacks and the broad, cure-all expectations that its founder has placed on the company's neural implant **incited increased scrutiny from regulators**. By contrast, however, other neurotech companies have, to date, managed largely to avoid such intense regulatory scrutiny.

These government investigations are probably the result of Musk's negative **Twitter "X" posts about President Biden's disastrous economic policies.** Also, Musk didn't want to work with the government because of bureaucracy. [96] [Editor's Note: before Trump 47.]

While Elon Musk has been busy taking over Twitter, Neuralink has been working on refining its technology, which is aimed at creating implants that allow a direct line of communication between the human brain and computers.

Called brain-computer interfaces, or BCIs for short, these systems use tiny electrodes placed in the brain to "read" signals from nearby neurons. Software then decodes these signals into commands or actions, such as moving a cursor or a robotic arm.

In a livestreamed "show and tell" event February 8, 2023, the Neuralink team presented improvements to its technology. Musk said that Neuralink had begun submitting paperwork for a human clinical trial to the Food and Drug Administration to implant a Neuralink device in a patient.

Musk revealed that the company's first two intended applications for its technology would be: **1. To help people with paralysis use their digital devices seamlessly; and, 2. To restore vision in those who have lost their eyesight.** [97]

Elon Musk says his ambitious plan to let humans wirelessly connect their brains with phones and other devices has taken a new step, announcing that **the first human received a brain implant from his Neuralink company in 2024.**

The person, who wasn't identified, "is recovering well." Neuralink's clinical trial is called PRIME—for Precise Robotically Implanted Brain-Computer Interface. As the name implies, **the process involves using a robot to** surgically insert the wires of the company's implant into a part of the brain related to movement.

Musk says patients will be outperforming pro gamers within two years: And that's not even his wildest claim. **Musk reckons Neuralink is going to have to speed up human brains so that AI doesn't get "bored."** [112]

Musk believes that "hundreds of millions" will have Neuralinks within "the next couple of decades."

FIXING NEUROLOGICAL DISORDERS

Computerizing a human brain could enable an unprecedented leap in treatment **...** *and even cure* complex neurological problems. **A BMI could potentially treat or cure depression, addiction, brain and spinal cord injuries ... and congenital defects.** [77]

And if you think isolated mini-brains—known formally as brain organoids—floating in a jar is creepy, upgrade your nightmares. **The next big thing in probing the brain is assembloids—free-floating brain circuits—that now combine brain tissue with an external output.** Because they're made of human tissue—often taken from actual human patients and converted into stem-cell-like states—organoids harbor the same genetic makeup as their donors. This makes it possible to study perplexing conditions such as autism, schizophrenia, or other brain disorders in a dish. [78]

With AI and Quantum Computing together by 2025, problem-solving abilities will go to a new dimension.

MILITARY ASPECTS

The military aspects of AI—combined with the synergistic aspects of singularity—are mind boggling. Not just regarding weapons, but also videos and images. For example, **China is the recognized leader in the emerging technique of Generative Adversarial Networks (GAN).**[63] Such as tricking computers into seeing objects in landscapes or satellite images that are NOT there. The concern, as AI technologists told *Quartz* in 2018, is that the same technique that can discern real bridges from fake ones, can also help to create fake bridges that AI cannot tell from the real.

Todd Myers, CIO at Office of the Director of Technology at the National Geospatial-Intelligence Agency, says, **"Forget about the Department of Defense and the Intelligence Community. Imagine Google Maps being infiltrated purposefully?"** Just one—or a few—of expertly manipulated data sets entered in an open-source image supply line via **GAN** could create havoc.

Recently **Open AI'**—artificial intelligence research laboratory—released its latest **GPT-3** (Generative Pre-trained Transformer 3**)** which is a classic example. It is considered the most powerful and revolutionary AI model that exists today. **It uses deep learning** (we will discuss this later) **to produce human-like text** to write news articles, student essays, blogs, computer code in any language and can generate pictures from the text. **There is no denying the potential dangers and harmful effects that lie with this technology** including fake news articles, misinformation, spam, fishing, social engineering and fraudulent academic essay writing.[74]

Information technology and computer power are growing exponentially. A key End Time scripture prophesying this is found in the Tanakh, in the *Book of Daniel*.

> *"But you, O Daniel, shut up the words, and seal the book, even to the time of the end: many shall run to and fro, and **knowledge shall be increased.**"* – Daniel 12:4

The Hebrew word for "knowledge" here used is "da-ath" and can also mean "discernment, understanding and wisdom" as well as "knowledge, perception and skill."

Technological singularity is credible. Therefore, we should consider not just its probability, but also its effect. It is estimated—**at today's rate of exponential technological growth**—that it will only take 25 Calendar Years to attain Technological Singularity. Ray Kurzwell projects:

*"To express this another way, it is not the case that we will experience a hundred years of progress in the twenty-first century; rather **we will witness on the order***

of twenty thousand years of progress (at today's rate of progress).[5]

Kurzweil, a renowned futurist and the director of engineering at Google, now says that the hardware needed to emulate the human brain may be ready even sooner than he predicted—in around 2020—using technologies such as graphics processing units (GPUs), which are ideal for brain-software algorithms. **He predicts that the complete brain software will take a little longer: until about 2029.** [Editor's Note: 75%?]

The implications of all this are mind-boggling. Shortly—about when the iPhone 19 is likely to be released—the smartphones in our pockets will be as computationally intelligent as we are. It doesn't stop there, though. **These devices will continue to advance, exponentially, until they exceed the combined intelligence of the human race.** Already, our computers have a big advantage over us: they are connected via the Internet and share information with each other billions of times faster than we can.[6]

Consider these aspects of increased research: chip speed, economics of production and other relevant matters will even **experience exponential growth 'in exponential growth.'**

However, here's a conundrum: What if, the HI's (Hyper Intelligences) are not easily manageable. If they are so far superior to human intelligence, **how can one**

presume that they can be controlled? Hypothetically, they could decide to: **1.** Eliminate humans; **2.** Use humans as slave-servants; **3.** Experiment with humans; **4.** Play with or torture humans; and, ultimately, **5. Behead humans for NOT taking the Mark of the Artificial Intelligence Avatar: The Image of the Beast.**

EDITOR'S COMMENT

I do NOT think that **by themselves**—by the computer HI's—the above five (5) options will be feasible. However, I do believe that **Artificial Intelligence (AI) via Hyper Intelligence Computers will be utilized by the False Messiah** (the anti-Christ) **and his False Prophet** (religious leader of the New Global Governance) **in the End Times**.

I believe that it is highly probable—not just possible, but probable—that **AI will be utilized in the personage of the IMAGE of the Beast in the End Times.**

IS YOUR JOB SAFE
WILL IT—*CAN IT*—BE REPLACED

Is YOUR job safe? Here are 5 unlikely industries that could be replaced by AI [82]

Writing ~ Even now, ChatGPT and similar technologies have the ability to write casual to professional speeches. They will be able to produce professional grade written content for any industry.

Research and Development ~ Google is rushing to integrate its own AI technology before being replaced by it. Already, **ChatGPT has astounding research capabilities**. If you type in any subject, it will produce an in-depth, nuanced analysis. Moreover, the technology has ability to improve upon itself, predict problems and produce solutions at a much faster rate than humans— and exponentially so. Can YOU do this?

Food Industry ~ AI will replace jobs in the food production industry AND chefs are already using AI to **predict food trends and manage food supply and prep.** There are AI robots under development that can produce faster, more efficiently, and with better quality and hygiene than humans—and with NO salary or perks!

Marketing ~ Beyond collecting data and predicting trends, ChatGPT is already able to generate unique marketing content based on those trends, from social media captions to email campaigns, based on the data it collects.

Academia ~ Students are using CHATGPT to write essays with good quality. Not only does AI have the ability to produce an incredibly in-depth summary of academic subjects with its own unique analysis but it won't be long before it is able to produce academic articles with pier-level academic integrity..

SO WHAT IS CHATGPT

"ChatGPT is a language model developed by OpenAI, designed to respond to text-based queries and generate natural language responses. It is part of the broader field of artificial intelligence known as natural language processing (NLP), which seeks to teach computers to understand and interpret human language.

ChatGPT is built using a deep learning architecture called the Transformer, which enables it to learn patterns in language and generate text that is coherent and human-like. It has been trained on a massive corpus of text data and can therefore generate responses to a wide variety of prompts, from general knowledge questions to more complex conversational topics.

One of the main applications of ChatGPT is in chatbots, where it can be used to provide automated customer service, answer FAQs, or even engage in more free-flowing conversations with users.

However, it can also be used in other NLP applications such as text summarization, language translation, and content creation."[84]

Introduction of ChatGPT ~ The initial model called ChatGPT interacted in a conversational way. The dialogue format made it possible for ChatGPT to answer follow-up questions, admit its mistakes, challenge incorrect premises, and reject inappropriate requests.[85]

For example, inputting "**explain how** the solar system was made" gave a more detailed result with more paragraphs than "**how was** the solar system made," even though both inquiries will give fairly detailed results. Taken a step further by giving ChatGPT more guidance about style or tone, saying "**explain how the solar system was made as a middle school teacher.**"

The basic version of ChatGPT was completely free to use. There's no limit to how much you could use ChatGPT in a day, though **there wss a word and character limit for responses.**

Dangers of CHATGPT ~ Arvind Narayanan, a computer science professor at Princeton, pointed out in a tweet: *"People are excited about using ChatGPT for learning. It's often very good. **But the danger is that you can't tell when it's wrong unless you already know the answer.** I tried some basic information security questions. In most cases the answers sounded plausible but were in fact BS."* [86]

Some "danger" items:

> Selfish humans[+++]
> Immoral
> Can write software … and malware
> Capable of being "sexist" and "racist"
> Convincing … even when it's wrong

[+++] I have seen an example of where ChatGPT **replied 'Selfish' humans 'deserve to be wiped out'** … but this response was flagged by Open Ai's systems as a possible violation of the company's content policy.

Paul Kedrosky (economist, venture capitalist and MIT fellow) says, *"Shame on OpenAI for launching this pocket nuclear bomb without restrictions into an unprepared society."* Wrote Kedrosky, *"I obviously feel ChatGPT (and its ilk) should be withdrawn immediately. And, if ever re-introduced, only with tight restrictions."*[87]

QUESTIONS: Will it be possible to distinguish between content that has been created by humans versus machines? Will we have to rely on machines to verify their own authenticity; if so, how can we trust them? Will ChatGPT cause interpersonal trust problems and higher suspicion? **What about when voice is introduced … introducing more potential for fraud?**

NOTE: Research through GPT-4 shows deep learning leverages more data and computation **to increasingly sophisticated and capable language models.**

SYNTHETIC BIOLOGY

Biological science is the field which deals with the production of "new life" patterns NOT existing in nature, resulting in synthetic organisms. Synthetic Biology is the design and construction of new biological parts, devices, and systems, and the re-design of existing, natural biological systems for *supposedly* useful purposes. **In 2010 there was a new type of life placed in artificial genetic material and chemically synthesized into cells that grew**. The life form was named Synthia.

DNA, or deoxyribonucleic acid, is the hereditary material in humans and almost all other organisms. The information in DNA is **stored as a code made up of four chemical bases**: adenine (A), guanine (G), cytosine (C), and thymine (T). The genetic code of organisms can now be read, and can be digitized into "0"s and "1"s in a computer database.[23]

Researchers at the University of Copenhagen are working on a **third strand of DNA**—a synthetic hybrid of protein and DNA—a tri-strand, which would be **"synthesizing life that is utterly alien to this world"** [and help them] "to put together a novel combination of molecules that can self-organize, metabolize, grow, reproduce and evolve."[24] Also, with a new groundbreaking technique, researchers from University of Copenhagen have managed to identify a protein that is responsible for cellular memory transmission when cells divide. **Cells divide constantly throughout life**. But **how do cells remember** whether to develop into skin, liver or intestinal cells? It's called epigenetic cellular memory.[64]

Inside the human cell, our DNA is wrapped around histone proteins. Together, they form a structure called chromatin. When a cell divides, it is crucial that both the DNA and the entire chromatin structure are copied accurately … and which genes are "turned on" and "off."

Recently, scientists have been able to extend lifespan in genetically diseased children affected by Progeria (due to a single letter change in the DNA). Most children with this disease do NOT live past 13 years, but the promise of synthetic biology should increase their lifespan by two and half times.[75]

An important property of DNA is that it can replicate or make copies of itself. This is critical when cells divide because each new cell needs to have an exact copy of the DNA present in the old cell. DNA is formed in two long strands that form a spiral called a double helix. Each strand of DNA in the double helix can serve as a pattern for duplicating the sequence of bases.

The question is—morally, ethically, medically and scientifically—**can we now originate life forms by reverse engineering**: from digital code to DNA and living cells? **What is the NEW definition of "human?"**

AI AND THE 4TH INDUSTRIAL REVOLUTION

THE NEW ARTIFICIAL INTELLIGENCE

WARNING: What you are about to learn will challenge your intellect. It will also enlighten you to "behind the scenes" activity that is happening today … and affecting your FUTURE.

We will discuss the 4th Industrial Revolution (IR-4) and WHY—unlike the previous three Industrial Revolutions—it will be dangerous.

People can lose their rights, their jobs … their lives. **Even more dangerous will be the result of our developing Artificial Intelligence (AI) that lives in Cyber Space that we do NOT really understand.**

The **4th Industrial Revolution** will be more of a **radical change than the first three … even though they were"shockers" in their inception.** Civilization has journeyed the route and use of fire, agriculture, the wheel, electricity, mass production, synthetic chemicals, the internet, block chain, self-driving cars, AI growing people in laboratories, and downloading our brains into computers.

Let's examine the first three Industrial Revolutions and see from whence we have journeyed.

FIRST INDUSTRIAL REVOLUTION ~ IR-1

The First Industrial Revolution was marked by a **transition from hand production methods to machines through the use of steam and water power**. The implementation of new technologies took a long time, so the period which this refers to was between 1760 and 1820, or 1840 in Europe and the United States.

SECOND INDUSTRIAL REVOLUTION ~ IR-2

The Second Industrial Revolution, also known as the Technological Revolution, is the period between 1871 and 1914 that resulted from **installations of extensive railroad and telegraph networks**, which allowed for faster transfer of people and ideas, **as well as electricity.** Increasing electrification allowed for factories to develop the modern production line.

THIRD INDUSTRIAL REVOLUTION ~ IR-3

The Third Industrial Revolution, also known as the Digital Revolution, occurred in the late 20th century. The production of the Z1 computer, which used **binary and Boolean logic**, was the beginning of more **advanced digital developments**. The next significant development in communication technologies was the **supercomputer**.

FOURTH INDUSTRIAL REVOLUTION ~ IR-4

The Fourth Industrial Revolution is the trend towards **automation and data exchange in manufacturing technologies and processes** which include **cyber-physical systems** (CPS), IoT, industrial **Internet of Things, cloud computing, cognitive computing,** and **artificial intelligence.**

The combination of machine learning and computational power allows machines to carry out highly complicated tasks. Also, in cooperation with Smart Factories.

NOTE: Computerization and digitalization were building blocks leading us to IR 4.0

The Smart Factory is no longer a vision. While different model factories represent the feasible, many enterprises already clarify with examples practically, how the Smart Factory functions.

The technical foundations on which the Smart Factory—**the intelligent factory**—is based are **cyber-physical systems** that communicate with each other using the Internet of Things and Services. An important part of this process is the **exchange of data between the product and the production line**. This enables a much more efficient connection of the Supply Chain and better organization within any production environment.

Within modular structured smart factories, cyber-physical systems monitor physical processes, create a virtual copy of the physical world and make decentralized decisions.

SO WHAT DOES THIS MEAN TO US

Artificial Intelligence has brought us a long way. However, **AI may take us too far**. The "danger zone" is when it will be able to think on the same level as a human. To develop a construct upon which to investigate, **let's examine the three different TYPES of AI.**

ARTIFICIAL INTELLIGENCE OR WEAK AI / ANI ~ NARROW INTELLIGENCE

Artificial intelligence is a computer system that can perform complex tasks that would otherwise require human minds—such as visual perception, speech recognition, decision-making, and translation between languages.

Most of these machines rely on **deep learning and programming**, which helps "teach" them to process vast amounts of data to **recognize patterns and carry out actions**. It is essentially recreating the human mind in machine form, similar to what is being carried out in Smart Factories today (as well as other areas of processing and bio-development).

Artificial Intelligence works on a supervised learning system, where various sets of data are provided to the machines, to learn from examples. This helps AI to classify objects or predict the results. AI performs intelligent tasks, but its reach is very narrow and limited as it can only provide an outcome that is already programmed. **It cannot make unpredictable decisions on its own, like a human brain can.**

AI is also referred to as Narrow AI [ANI] or Weak AI. This type of artificial intelligence is one that focuses primarily on one **single narrow task, with a limited range of abilities.** If you think of an example of AI that exists in our lives right now, it is ANI.

AGI – ARTIFICIAL GENERAL INTELLIGENCE OR TRUE (REAL) INTELLIGENCE

AGI technology would be **on the level of the human mind.** Due to this fact, it will probably be some time before we truly grasp AGI, as we still don't know all there is to know about the human brain itself. However, in concept at least, AGI would be **able to think on the same level as a human,** much like Sonny the robot in **I-Robot featuring Will Smith.**

Artificial General Intelligence, on the contrary, is the intelligence of a machine that could perform all the intellectual tasks performed by human beings. It possesses **the ability to analyze a situation on its own and take a calculative decision,** like humans can, **without having to be programmed in advance. We are actually nearing that in some of our Smart Factories.** As I noted previously, within modular structured Smart Factories, cyber-physical systems

62

monitor physical processes, create a virtual copy of the physical world and make decentralized decisions.

ASI – ARTIFICIAL SUPER INTELLIGENCE

This is where it gets a little theoretical and a touch scary. **ASI refers to AI technology that will match and then surpass the human mind**. To be classed as an ASI, **the technology would have to be more capable than a human in every single way possible**. Not only could these AI things carry out tasks, but they would even be capable of having emotions and relationships.

NOTE: <u>The evolution from AGI to ASI would in theory be much faster than it is taking us to get from ANI to AGI right now</u>, since **AGI would allow computers to "think" and exponentially improve themselves once they are able to really learn from experience and by trial and error.** If a transition to ASI ever happens, the exponential growth that is in theory expected to occur at this point is often called an **Intelligence Explosion … SINGULARITY!**

NOTE: We should ensure a safe and ethical functioning of AI in all fields and make it a priority in further development. However, once systems start "thinking" on their own—**with NO knowledge of God**—what are the limits?!

WHAT ABOUT NEW GLOBAL GOVERNANCE

The future Global Leader (the FALSE mashiach) … **along with his False Prophet … will demand the**

populace to take a digital "mark" on their right hands or forehead that will "connect" them with a Smart System without which they can neither BUY nor SELL.

ARE YOU READY FOR THIS

▶ Brain modification allowing receptors to gain access to—or receive messages from—paranormal and Satanic occult sources.

▶ Downloading—via the transfer of artificial intelligence (AI) information—through brain-machine interfacing, a desire for the "Mark of the Beast."

▶ Corrupted spermatozoa which could fertilize an ovum producing a hybrid being: a non—other than normal—human life form.

▶ Receiving fallen—demonically anointed—influence via psycho-neural pathways.

SUMMARY

I have alerted you to what the New Global Governance Leader—Antichrist—FALSE messiah will use in the End Times. Teach AND prepare your children and grandchildren about what is and will be happening. Make sure that YOU and your progeny are prepared for Heaven.

TO LUST OR NOT TO LUST
AFTER GRIN

As discussed earlier, **genetic engineering is a biotechnological application where the DNA or genes of organisms are manipulated according to the requirement.**

Genetic engineering is any process by which genetic material (**the building blocks of heredity**) is changed in such a way as to make possible the production of new substances or new functions. As an example, biologists have now learned how to transplant the gene that produces light in a firefly into tobacco plants. The function of that gene—the production of light—has been added to the normal list of functions of the tobacco plants.

If genes are chemical compounds, then they can be manipulated just as any other kind of chemical compound can be manipulated. Since DNA molecules are very large and complex, the actual task of manipulation may be difficult. However, the principles involved in working with DNA molecule genes are no different than the research principles with which all chemists are familiar.

It should be obvious that enzymes such as these can be used by scientists as submicroscopic scissors and glue with which one or more DNA molecules can be cut apart, rearranged, and the put back together again.[9]

CRISPR technology is a simple yet powerful tool for editing genomes. **It allows researchers to easily alter DNA sequences and modify gene function.** Many potential applications include correcting genetic defects, treating and preventing the spread of diseases and improving crops. However, its promise also raises ethical concerns.

NOTE: CRISPR components can cut DNA at desired locations [if 100% precise] but the cell's repair mechanisms also play an important role in enabling changes to the genetic code.[65]

CRISPR" (pronounced "crisper") is shorthand for "CRISPR-Cas9." **CRISPRs are specialized stretches of DNA.** The protein Cas9 (or "CRISPR-associated") is **an enzyme that acts like a pair of molecular scissors, capable of cutting strands of DNA.**

CRISPR is it is not one hundred percent efficient. There is also the phenomenon of **"off-target effects,"** where DNA is cut at sites **other than the intended target**. This can lead to the introduction of unintended mutations … plus the effects of NOT getting a "precise" edit.

THINK ABOUT THIS

According to scientist Bill Joy, Co-Founder of Sun Microsystems, GRIN Tech—genetic engineering, robotics, artificial intelligence and nanotechnology— presents **"a different threat than the technologies that have come before. Specifically, robots, engineered organisms, and nanobots share a dangerous amplifying factor. They can self-replicate. A bomb is blown up only once—but one bot can become many, and quickly get out of control."**

There are now annual synthetic biology symposiums attended by college students. One is iGEM— International Genetically Engineered Machine. The iGEM Foundation is dedicated to education and competition, **advancement of synthetic biology, and the development of open community and collaboration**.

iGEM runs the premiere student competition in Synthetic Biology. Student teams are given a kit of biological parts and work over the summer to build biological systems and operate them in living cells. In 2009, the iGEM winners formulated **E. chromi**, a version of food poisoning bacteria.

Companies like SYNTHEGO offer "Engineered Cells" and "CRISPR Revolution Kits."[66]

GRIN technology does NOT require large warehouses or manufacturing plants—or resources—to create implements of mass destruction ... PLUS ... the ability for multiplicative reproduction. Add to this the **open source availability on the internet of formulae and instructions on HOW to make deadly viruses capable of mass destruction that can be utilized by terrorists**.

GRIN, GEOPOLITICS & GLOBAL GUIDES

We are at the threshold of **the most cataclysmic— the worst and most evil—change in society** that Planet Earth has ever known.

This change is at the same time malevolent and opaque. You will NOT see through it—**without revelation**—which is WHY God crossed our paths. He sent me to help you comprehend both its vastness and viciousness.

I'm NOT talking about the New World Order—Global Governance—although that's a small part of it. I'm talking about **something so sinister—and at the same time—so appealing to every thinking person**.

I'm talking about something that has its "core association" in age-old Biblical history but—*at this moment*—is on the cutting edge of science and technology.

Don't be mistaken! Even though the triad of **government, military and education is spending millions of dollars in R & D**—with the financial support of banks and corporations—there is an unseen, dark force behind the "push" forward.

But … here is something even more amazing! There is also *at this time* a hidden geopolitical "behind–the-scenes" amalgamation—a spiritual collusion—both human and other-worldly that is being orchestrated to facilitate control … of YOU and your family.

Don't worry about being left behind at the appearing of Messiah—that is, IF you KNOW Him. **What you need to worry about NOW is**:

- Being left behind by enhanced humans.

- Being tempted to sacrifice your autonomy.

- Being "setup" to lose your children's DNA.

- Being handed over to the Global Citizenry.

Thinking it's not possible? Then … **you NEED to know the interconnection of the Mystery Matrix.** I have mentioned the Mystery Matrix previously and we will cover it fully later in the book. However, **I do want to discuss at this point—in the next section—the Matrix as it relates to Israel and the End Times.**

ISRAEL: 3 STRIKES AND YOU'RE IN

Israel—whether realizing it or not—is going to win a major conquest over Muslim nations in the Middle East. And not just win … but plunder them, reaping great resources! No, I am NOT talking about the Ezekiel 38 – 39 Victory. I am talking about a conquest even before that: one that could happen at any time. Actually, **there will be at least three (3) major Middle East conflicts that involve Israel in the future**:

- Conquest over Muslim forces in Middle East;

- Ezekiel 38 – 39 victory; and,

- Battle of Armageddon. (The above two may be incorporated in this one … all three the same

CONQUEST OVER MUSLIM ENTITIES
STRIKE #1

Most people familiar with Bible prophecy realize there will be a conflict in the Middle East—fought in Israel—where God Himself will be "set apart" in the eyes of the goyim: the nations. That is, when it is over, the whole world will realize that the conflict has been won by the LORD God.

And, some of the people familiar with this prophecy in Ezekiel Chapters 38 and 39 believe that it is **NOT the same conflict as the Battle of Armageddon**. This fact is seems on the surface to be valid in that:

- The weapons used are different.

- The enemies involved are different.

In addition, when the conflict of Ezekiel 38 and 39 happens, **Israel is at peace in the land with great resources**. Even a casual reading of Ezekiel Chapter 38 shows that **Israel's great wealth will be what draws the powers from the North to come down against her**. This brings to light another question: Where—and when—did Israel come by this great wealth?!

The Middle East conflict … the Israeli-Arab dispute … is at its essence thousands of years old. **It is a spiritual conflict**: the political aspects of which are merely the symptoms.

The scriptures do show us that there will be a future Israeli-Arab war.

PSALM 83

In Psalm 83 we see what **MAY BE** a parallel description of Isaiah Chapter Eleven—**possibly**—in more detail as it pertains to the parties involved. Remember, the *Book of Isaiah* was written more recently, around 750 BCE … while *Psalm 83* was written about 1,000 BCE around King David's reign. However, the Spirit of God can use writers, including prophets, at different times of writing to make declarations **concerning the same events**: even future. However, **Psalm 83 is NOT a prophecy**.

"Keep not silence, O God: hold not your peace, and be not still, O God.

For, behold, your enemies make a tumult: and they that hate you have lifted up the head.

They have taken crafty counsel against your people (Israel) and consulted against your hidden ones.

They have said, **'Come, and let us cut them off from being a nation; that the name of Israel may be no more in remembrance.'**

For they have consulted together with one consent: they are confederate against you:

The tabernacles of Edom, and the Ishmaelites; of Moab, and the Hagarenes;

Gebal, and Ammon, and Amalek; the Philistines with the inhabitants of Tyre;

Assur also is joined with them: they have helped the children of Lot. Selah." – Psalm 83:1-8

For a description of the cognate terms listed in the above passage and their current identity, the following will help:

The tabernacles, or tents, of Edom are Israel's traditional enemies: the Palestinians and other political Arab allies: Gaza, the West Bank and Golan Heights.

Esau represents Mount Seir from the Dead Sea south to the Red Sea (Eilat and Gulf of Aqaba).

The **Ishmaelites** were not confined to the descendants of the son of Abraham and Hagar, but refer to the desert tribes east of the Jordan River, in general, like "t"e children of the east" "Judges 7:12) … but also in the Arabian Desert.

The **Gebalites** were predominantly in or near the area of Lebanon. (Joshua 13:15)

The **Hagarenes**: Hagar was Abraham's maid who gave birth to his first child, Ishmael (the son of the 'flesh,' not the 'promise.'). Hagar gave her son, Ishmael, to an Egyptian wife so that the Ishmaelites,or **Hagarenes**, of Gilead and Moab were three-quarters Egyptian.

Asshur represents the ancient confines of Assyria (present day Syria and Iraq) plus Turkey.

NOTICE: The people groups and nations listed in Psalm 83 who want Israel's destruction are ALL presently Muslim entities.

ISAIAH CHAPTER 11

In Isaiah Chapter 11, verses 12-16, we read a description of **a war that will happen BEFORE Messiah comes to earth again (the second time)**. The first 11 verses tell us about Messiah's'return and his rule of peace on earth. Verses 12-16 (the description of war) cannot happen during this time because Messiah's'reign is characterized by peace. **Another distinctive feature** of the prophecy in verses 12-16 is that **the war therein described has NOT happened historically. It has not happened yet!**

A war between Israel and probably all of the Middle East MAY happen, not just bordering Arab states like Lebanon, Syria, and Jordan. They (that is, **the children of Israel** ..doesn'toth Ephraim and Judah) will

75

"f"y down upon the shoulder of the Philistines (Palestinians) to the west"." In context Israel will strike against Egypt and Iraq (Assyria) and **"p"under the sons of the East"."** Israel will control these nations, and evidently, their wealth as a result of the plundering. Etymologically, the **"p"ople of the East" "nclude** the Arab nations of **Saudi Arabia, Yemen, Kuwait, Bahrain, UAE, and others**.

It is very evident her" in this passage .". see verse 14 ... that **Israel will control the East Bank of Jordan (Ammon, Moab, and Edom)**. This happened in Joshua's'time and **it has NOT happened SINCE the days of Isaiah. This is a future prophecy that WILL happen! Maybe before Armageddon!**

It is quite probable that the devastation of terrorist groups like Al-Aqsa Martyrs Brigade, Hamas, Fatah, Al-Qaeda and ISIS will be accomplished during this conflict. **It may be one of the factors—if not the primary factor—that precipitates the conflict**. Actually, many of the citizens in these Muslim nations may be glad Israel wins this conflict to deliver them from the hands of terrorist groups and leadership.

So now we know what the "hook" is that God uses to draw the powers from the North.

> *"I will turn you back, and **put hooks into your jaws**, and I will bring you forth ..."* – Ezekiel 38:4

"I will go to them that are at rest, that dwell safely, all of them dwelling without walls, and having neither bars nor gates,

To take a spoil, and to take a prey; to turn your hand upon the desolate places that are now inhabited, and upon the people that are gathered out of the nations." – Ezekiel 38:11-12

Remember, Isaiah Chapter Eleven verse 14 tells us, *"Israel will strike against Egypt and Assyria (Iraq and Syria) and "p"under the sons of the East"."* Israel will control these nations, and evidently, their wealth as a result of the plundering.

This explains where—and when—Israel achieves **the great wealth that God will use to draw the powers from the North against her**. Notice, also, that these entities that are conquered by Israel are ALL Muslim nations.

So, who are these powers from the North that come against Israel to take a spoil? They are the ones who are involved in Strike #2: the Ezekiel 38 – 39 victory for Israel.

EZEKIEL 38-39 VICTORY
STRIKE #2

In Ezekiel Chapter 38, there is NO mention of Israel's neighbors joining in allegiance with the powers from the North. **NO mention of:**

- Lebanon
- Egypt
- Saudi Arabia
- Syria
- Jordan
- Iraq
- Palestinians

The conflict described in Ezekiel Chapters 38 and 39 involves the powers from the North.

*"Son of man, set your face against **Gog, the land of Magog, the chief prince of Meshech and Tubal**, and prophesy against him,*

*And say, This is what the Lord GOD says; Behold, I am against you, **O Gog, the chief prince of Meshech and Tubal**:*

And I will turn you back, and put hooks into your jaws, and I will bring you forth, and all your army, horses and horsemen, all of them clothed with all sorts of armor, even a great company with bucklers and shields, all of them handling weaponry:

Persia, Ethiopia, and Libya with them*; all of them with shield and helmet:*

Gomer, and all his bands; the house of Togarmah of the north quarters, and all his bands*: and many people with you."* – Ezekiel 38:2-6

NOTICE: Magog is a people group, while Gog is a Satanically inspired leader of that people.

Wilhelm Gesenius was a renowned German Biblical critic and pioneer of critical Hebrew lexicography and grammar. Here is his analysis of the "movers and shakers" in this passage.

> *"Meshech was a barbarous people known as Moschi who dwelt in the Moschian mountains; the root from which the city of Moscow [derived] its name."*

However, **Mushki (MŠK) of central and western Asia Minor,** known in the classics (Homer, etc.) as Phrygia, fits very well. **These people were well known to Ezekiel, and this may be the easier interpretation**

We know that Persia is synonymous with present day Iran.

Tubal, Gomer and Togarmah represent sections of Turkey.

● WHAT IS EZEKIEL SAYING TODAY

Read carefully Ezekiel Chapters 38 and 39. Then compare what you have read with the following synopsis. I think you will agree.

> ■ Turkey, Iran and other Middle East and North East African nations—along with possibly the southern steppes of Russia—will form an alliance to attack Israel.

> ■ God will defeat this alliance of Magog and others on the hills of Israel, and leave only 17 percent of them.

> ■ It will take seven months to bury the dead bodies, and seven years to burn the implements of war (probably radioactive elements).

> ■ The **victory for Israel will be so great** and miraculous that **ALL nations will realize that the God of Israel is the LORD**.

"Thus says the Lord GOD; Are you, Gog, the one of whom I have spoken in old time by my servants the prophets of Israel, which prophesied in those days many years that I would bring you against them?

And it shall come to pass at the same time when Gog shall come against the land of Israel, says the Lord GOD, that my fury shall come up in my face.

*For in my jealousy and in the fire of my wrath have I spoken, Surely in that day there shall be a **great shaking in the land of Israel;***

So that the fish of the sea, and the birds of the heaven, and the beasts of the field, and all creeping things that creep upon the earth, and all the men that are upon the face of the earth, shall shake at my presence, and the mountains shall be thrown down, and the steep places shall fall, and every wall shall fall to the ground.

*And I will call for a sword against him throughout all my mountains, says the Lord GOD: **every man's'weapon shall be against his brother.***

*And I will plead against him with **pestilence and with blood**; and I will rain upon him, and upon his bands, and upon the many people that are with him, an overflowing **rain, and great hailstones, fire, and brimstone.***

This is how I will magnify myself, and sanctify myself; and I will be known in the eyes of many nations, and they shall know that I am the LORD.*" –
Ezekiel 38:18-23

PLAYERS IN ALIGNMENT AGAINST ISRAEL

Think about this: the players today in alignment against Israel are the same as mentioned in Ezekiel Chapters 38 and 39. We know this because of the cognate forms of names used in the original Hebrew. The only difference is ... they have NOT attacked yet.

Magog—Possibly the Southern Steppes of Russia (former Soviet- Bloc countries); but <u>for sure</u> **Turkey**;

Meshech—Central and Western Asia (and part of **Turkey**);

Tubal—**Turkey**;

Persia—Iran;

Ethiopia—Southern Egypt, Sudan, Somalia;

Libya—Libya (may also include Algeria, Morocco, and Tunisia);

Gomer—North-Central **Turkey**;

Togarmah—Eastern **Turkey**.

The Triumvirate of Testing for Israel at this moment is: Russia, Iran, and Turkey. Russia cavorts with whomever, always seeking the balance of power: its own. Iran wants to exterminate anyone the Mad Mahdi doesn't'approve, which happens to be ALL non-Muslims. And **Turkey, is coming out of the closet, in preparation for her role as the headquarters for New World Governance**. Watch Turkey!

RUSSIA

Russia has been attempting to attach its holdings in previous Soviet Bloc countries to prevent NATO encroachment into these areas. It was strategically taking advantage of the recent American president's'(Obama) weakness in military experience and foreign policy negotiations. [Editor's Note: It is possible that Russia will NOT be involved due to etymological usage of the word "Rosh" in Ezekiel's "time-context."]

IRAN

Iran wants to fill the void in the Middle East which resulted from the invasion of Iraq. (This also happens to be a goal of Turkey.) Iran, under the leadership of the Grand Meany and his puppet Barney Fife want to bring destruction and chaos to ALL non-Muslim people and nations.

Iran now has the capability to produce a nuclear weapon. It has warhead capability.

The MAJOR reason Iran is NOT attacking Israel right now is to give Iran TIME to produce several bombs first. In the past Iran knew that USA President Obama had NO military background and was without experience in war strategy or military diplomacy. Iran felt USA president Obama was weak and would easily be dissuaded with rhetoric, **using his Muslim upbringing as a tool on the chessboard.**

Iran seeks to gain BOTH **time** and **privilege.** Both are a bonus toward their efforts. After using the previous USA Presidents Obama and Biden and after gaining hard assets and other desirables earned via diplomacy, Iran was left with an even better position to attack Israel.

If, however, NO advantageous benefits are to be realized from the USA, Iran can still attack Israel; all the while having created a situation of non-apprehension while creating more bombs. Here are some recent timelines:

March 3, 2020 – In a report to member states, and obtained by CNN, the IAEA says that Tehran's stockpiles of low enriched uranium now far exceed 300 kilograms, the limit set by the 2015 Iran nuclear deal. The report notes that Iran has nearly tripled its stockpile of low enriched uranium since November 2019, indicating a significant jump in production.

November 27, 2020 – According to Iran's semi-official news agency, ISNA, Iran's top nuclear scientist Mohsen Fakhrizadeh was killed in an apparent assassination. Fakhrizadeh was head of the research center of new technology in the Revolutionary Guards, and was a leading figure in Iran's nuclear program.

December 2, 2020 – Iran's parliament passes a bill that would boost uranium enrichment to pre-2015 levels and block nuclear inspections if sanctions are not lifted, in the wake of the assassination of Fakhrizadeh.

January 4, 2021 – Iran announces that it had resumed enriching uranium to 20% purity, far beyond the limits laid out in the 2015 nuclear deal, in a move likely to further escalate tensions with the United States. Iran was banking on the soft underbelly—and easily swayed sentiment—of Joe Biden.

2023 – Iranian authorities face considerable challenges at home in terms of the economy, as the unrest and a number of strikes tied to the protests have only piled on the pressure that US and Western sanctions effected.

If the United States doesn't reenter the 2015 nuclear deal it abandoned and/or Iran doesn't come back into compliance with the terms of the agreement, then **expect talk of war to grow**. In such a scenario, Iran would want to have demonstrated that a fight wouldn't be easy for the U.S. or Israel to win. **So Iran is helping Russia in the Ukraine conflict with drones**.

Iranians are in Crimea to help Russia and Tehran has given Moscow "dozens" of drones to date. Russia *"will likely continue to receive additional shipments in the future."* [99] According to Tanakh, the Prophet Ezekiel (Chapters 38 and 39) describes a military bond between Iran and Russia and Turkey (plus two Northeast African countries) to attack Israel when the land is at peace.

WHY? Because of Israel's future wealth. The powers of the North will try unsuccessfully to plunder Israel. The LORD will WIN the battle! Eighty-three percent (83%) of the enemy forces will die on Israeli soil.

October 7, 2023 – President Biden gave billions of USD$ to Iran which Iran then used to finance nuclear development PLUS terrorist activities in Hamas, Hezbollah, Yemen (Houthis) and elsewhere … and **which financed the horrific terrorist attacks by Hamas against Israel on October 7th, 2023.**

September 17 & 18, 2024 – The Secrets Behind Hezbollah's Beeper Explosion.

The operation began 10 years before when **Mossad developed walkie-talkies with hidden explosive devices in their batteries.**

Mossad—The Institute—clandestinely sold over 16,000 walkie-talkies to Hezbollah. The walkie-talkies were primarily being used in battle situations, but Mossad wanted a smaller device Hezbollah members would always carry. **They focused on pagers.**

Even the saleswoman Hezbollah was accustomed to working with was recruited, offering the first batch of 5,000 pagers as a free upgrade.

On September 17, 2023, at 3:30 PM, the pagers simultaneously beeped across Lebanon and then exploded. Hezbollah was caught completely off guard as hospitals filled with injured members— some missing fingers or limbs, others blinded, and some with severe internal injuries. Mossad mostly achieved its goal of targeting terrorists while leaving bystanders unharmed.

The next day, Mossad activated the dormant walkie-talkies, some exploding during funerals for the pager victims.

December 2024 – See *"So What Happened in Syria"* below and HOW it affected Iran, Russia and Turkey … as well as Israel.

TURKEY

Iran, Russia and Turkey met July, 2022, in Tehran as **Partners, Competitors and Opponents**. The leaders of ALL these three countries have disagreements with the USA and Israel. What did they hope to accomplish as a result of these meetings?

All three nations conflicted on Syria. All three countries have made statements in the past concerning their views of a New World Order.

The REAL "Elephant in the Room" was NOT even mentioned by major media ... even Christian media! All three of these countries are MAJOR PLAYERS in the future attack on Israel.

Turkey has in recent years been anti-Iran—anti-Shia—because Turkey has 90% Sunni Muslims versus 10% Shia (Iran is Shia). But recently Turkey is warming up to Iran. WHY? Turkey suffered massive power cuts to industrial customers in January 2022 at an unprecedented level never seen before after the country's **natural gas supplies dipped following a disruption of imports from Iran.**

There is also the issue of which country takes LEADERSHIP in becoming the regional hub in terms of transit routes (land, rail and energy). **Turkey is working on the so-called "Middle Corridor" (from China to Central Asia, Caucasus, Turkey and on into Europe).** Iran is trying to work its way through Russia to its north and the areas to its south.

However, the BIG KEY in all these meetings was the diplomacy and relationships of the three countries to cajole with one another. WHY? **They have one "hidden" goal: to defeat and control Israel. They want the wealth of Israel. And in the not to far-off future they will desire it even more!** See *Israel's'Future Wealth* [107] by Prince Handley.

According to the Prophet Ezekiel, **Turkey** (Togarmah) will one day ally itself with the Islamic confederation led by **Iran** (Persia) and will also join forces with **Russia** as a participant in the Gog-Magog War.

When you see these three (3) forces—Turkey, Iran and Russia—meeting and planning together, it is ONE MORE STEP forward towards a tripartite cohesion for an attack on Israel. Just as Ezekiel prophesied, Russia, Turkey, and Iran will one day align to form a confederacy (with others) to attack Israel. (Read Ezekiel Chapters 38 and 39.) **This Ezekiel 38-39 conflict <u>does NOT have to be in the core of the End Times</u>. It MAY be—and could be—well before Armageddon!**

NOTE ALSO: An attack against Israel from Iran MAY be well BEFORE the conflict of Ezekiel Chapters 38 and 39!

One item of super interest between the three countries was Syria. Russia and Iran were against any purported plans by Turkey tor military action in Northern Syria which is at Turkey's'border. **Also, Iran's presence in Syria was more visible until December 2024**. Iran wanted to keep its influence in Syria, maintain the connection with Iraq, and **keep the Shia Belt running from Iran to Lebanon**.

SO, WHAT HAPPENED IN SYRIA

Half a century of rule by the Assad family in Syria crumbled with astonishing speed after insurgents burst out of a rebel-held enclave and converged on the capital, Damascus, taking city after city in a matter of days. [108]

The overthrow of Syria's 24 year autocrat President Bashar al-Assad in December 2024 with the resulting ousting of KEY Iranian and Russian military installations changes the whole scenery in Syria.

It is a "game-changer" for Israel. The Assad regime was an ally of the Islamic Republic of Iran, and a part of the latter's so-called Axis of Resistance against Israel. In a message to the new regime taking shape in Syria, Prime Minister Benjamin Netanyahu said that Israel wants to establish relations, but won't hesitate to attack if it threatens the Jewish state.

"We have no intention of interfering in the internal affairs of Syria," he said in a video statement, *"but we certainly do intend to do what is necessary to ensure our security."*

Therefore, he said, the Israeli Air Force was bombing **military strategic capabilities** left by the Syrian military of the ousted Assad regime, ***"so that they won't fall into the hands of the jihadists."*** [109]

THE ROLE OF TURKEY IN PROPHECY

A while back, Turkey's President Recep Tayyip Erdogan entered the two golden gates of the Kaaba in Mecca, Saudi Arabia. The Kaaba ("The Cube") also referred as Al Kaaba Al Musharrafah (The Holy Kaaba), is a building at the center of Islam's'most sacred mosque, Al-Masjid al-Haram, **in Mecca**, al-Hejaz, Saudi Arabia. It is the most sacred Muslim site in the world.

Erdogan wanted to be the protector of Mecca and Medina where he is currently working with the Saudi King alongside an alliance of ten Muslim states. Al-Tahaluf Al-A'shari, literally the **Ten Nation Confederacy** which the media in English calls "Ten Sunni-led Arab States" was established in response to the U.S. abandonment of Saudi Arabia and a response to Iran's threat to the region, the Sunni Muslim world has risen to form a major unified force.

The anti-Christ (the Beast) or **FALSE messiah—NOT the REAL Mashiach**—MAY come from the geopolitical confines of any of the following areas: Turkey, the Mediterranean, including North Africa and the Middle East.

So, with all this geopolitical alignment of nations against Israel—*not counting all the other nations*—it's plain to

91

see that Ezekiel was a watchman for Israel in his day, **but more importantly for today** … and for the future.

And … after the Ezekiel 38-39 conflict, there will be **a third major conflict**—a third strike, if you will—and it will NOT be "3 strikes and you're out." It will be **for Israel, "3 strikes and you're in … for good!"** This third major conflict will be what is known as **the Battle of Armageddon**.

As we discussed previously, a war between Israel and probably ALL the Middle East will happen, not just bordering Arab states like Lebanon, Syria, and Jordan. Israel will *"fly down upon the shoulder of the Philistines (the Palestinians) to the west."*

In context Israel will strike against Egypt and Iraq (Assyria) and "plunder the people of the East**." Israel will CONTROL these nations, and evidently their WEALTH because of the plundering.**

Etymologically, the "people of the East" include the Arab nations of Saudi Arabia, Yemen, Kuwait, Bahrain, UAE, and others.

It is very evident here (in this passage) that Israel will CONTROL the East Bank of Jordan (Ammon, Moab, and Edom). This happened in Joshua's time and has NOT happened SINCE the days of Isaiah. This is a future prophecy that WILL happen!

This position of prosperity and power will be part of the "hook" in the jaw that God uses to draw the powers from the North (Russian, Turkey, Iran and two Northeastern African nations) to wage war against Israel.

REPEAT: The extreme wealth that Israel will control will be one of the things God uses to draw the northern confederacy described in Ezekiel. (See the Tanakh: Ezekiel 38:4-5, 39:2 and Ezekiel 38:10-12.

Many people, some scholars, confuse the Battle of Armageddon with the conflict described in Ezekiel Chapters 38 and 39. **Some wrongfully associate these battles with the same.** They may NOT be the same battles because of the following:

▪ The people being defeated are different.

▪ The weapons being used to win are different.

▪ The attacks are against different parties.

NOTICE: Watch for a **NEW Ottoman Empire** to arrive with a revised **Islamic Caliphate from Turkey**.

THE PEOPLE DEFEATED ARE DIFFERENT

■ In the Battle of Armageddon **ALL the nations** of the earth are involved.

■ In the battle described in Ezekiel 38-39 the people who join themselves to fight against Israel are confederates of **the power with the North** (Russia, Turkey, Iran and their confederates) along with allies from northeast Africa. Note: direction in the Bible is always in relation to Jerusalem.

THE WEAPONS USED ARE DIFFERENT

■ In the Battle of Armageddon a sword proceeds from the mouth of the Lord and destroys the kings and peoples of ALL nations that would choose to fight against Him (those deceived by Satan). The Holy Bible teaches that a "g"eat lie","a delusion, will be sent upon the earth by Satan in the last days.

■ In Ezekiel Chapter 38 the weaponry the Lord uses are earthquake(s), disease, flooding rain, hailstones, fire and brimstone. Also, God will cause the enemies of Israel to fight among themselves.

94

ATTACKS ARE AGAINST DIFFERENT PARTIES

■ In the Battle of Armageddon the attack is against the LORD: the Mashiach of Israel.

■ In Ezekiel the attack is against Israel.

Notice that it is **God that draws the enemy from the north** (Russia) and her allies (Iran, Turkey and others). **God puts "hooks" in their jaws and leads them out with their armies."** (Ezekiel 38:4-5, 39:2)

Also, any of the following reasons God might use to draw the northern power(s) at this present time:

■ Israel's present wealth;

■ Israel's scientific superiority;

■ Israel's strategic geo-military positioning;

■ Israel's previous victories over Islamic / Aabic factions.

THE BATTLE OF ARMAGEDDON
STRIKE # 3
ISRAEL: 3 STRIKES AND YOU'RE IN

In the Battle of Armageddon, the kings of the earth, and of the whole world, are gathered together to the battle of that great day of God Almighty. [Revelation 16:12-16]

These kings of the earth and people from the whole world will be drawn to battle by three (3) demons (unclean spirits) that come out of the mouths of:

■ The dragon (Satan, the devil);

■ The beast (the False Messiah, or anti-Christ); and,

■ The false prophet (the New World Order—or New Global Governance—religious leader).

The Battle of Armageddon will involve ALL the nations of the earth. The Beast (who will be the False Messiah), the kings of the earth, and their armies gather to make war against Yeshua (Jesus) the Messiah.

The Beast and the False Prophet are captured in this war and BOTH are cast alive into the lake that burns with fire and brimstone. The rest of the people will be killed with a sword (probably the Word of God), which proceeds from the mouth of Messiah.

Satan, the devil, will be bound for 1,000 years in the bottomless pit (during the millennial reign of Messiah). At the end of the 1,000-year reign of Messiah on earth, Satan will be cast alive into the Lake of Fire where the Beast and the False Prophet—who have already been there for 1,000 years—have been tormented. Then, **all three will be tormented for** *"time upon time, with NO end."* Plus, all the people who have rejected Messiah's love and GIFT of salvation will be tormented forever, because they have neglected their only eternal hope.

There will be an earthly Kingdom established after the great war where Messiah wipes out all the enemies of Israel in the Battle of Armageddon. Immediately after, the Messiah will rule from Jerusalem. All ethnic groups (goyim) remaining and their leaders must be subservient to the King.

Now that we have a perspective of key End Time waymarks, **let us discuss the interconnectivity of the Mystery Matrix with Israel.**

SOME INFORMATION ON CHINA

China and India will probably be part of the **King's of the East** that Brit Chadashah (New Testament) talks about concerning the End Times (see Revelation 16:12).

However, these are NOT part of the End Time 10 kings who side with the FALSE mashiach (the coming world dictator prophesied by Daniel). Why? Because **China & India existed before and during the time of Yochanan's prophecy in Revelation Chapter 17.**

For more information on the **End Time Ten Kings**, see Price Handley's teaching: *"Israel: Daniel Warned You About the Ten Kings."* [107]

"And the ten horns which you saw are ten kings, which have received NO kingdom as yet; but receive power as kings one hour with the beast. These have one mind and shall give their power and strength unto the beast." Revelation 17:12-13

"I wouldn't call it a true full alliance in the real meaning of that word, but we are seeing them [Russia and China] moving closer together, and that's troublesome," Chairman of the Joint Chiefs of Staff, Gen.Milley, said. *"And then ... Iran is the third.*[100]

Turkey is seeking membership to the China-led Shanghai Cooperation Organization as President Recep Tayyip Erdogan attempts to forge alliances with friendly countries in the East.[101]

REMEMBER: All three of these—**Russia, Iran and Turkey—will one day attack Israel and lose five-sixths (83%) of their forces inside the land of Israel.** Total defeat! **All the world will know that the LORD won the battle!** (Ezekiel 38:23)

Read Ezekiel Chapters 38 and 39.

NOTE: Newer versions of the Holy Bible do NOT include *"and leave but the sixth part of you"* from Ezekiel 39:2.

INTERCONNECTIVITY OF THE
MYSTERY MATRIX WITH ISRAEL

So now that you know the sequence of the Three Strikes—the three major conflicts involving Israel—let's discuss HOW the Mystery Matrix connects to Israel. We will NOT go into the details of the Mystery Matrix at this time: that is later in the book. However, we will give a brief glimpse of the clandestine goals of this Evil Enterprise.

Who would—and WHY would they—want to destroy Israel? Prince Handley has often said that Israel's motto should be: **"Attack me again … I need the real estate!"**

First, let's discuss **the originator—the primal cause and energy—of the Mystery Matrix**, and later in the book we will discuss how GRIN plus other "out of this world" players fit into the outcroppings of the Mystery Matrix.

The architect of the Mystery Matrix is none other than Satan, that old serpent: the devil. Let's look at some of the reasons he is behind the attacks on Israel … and WHY he hates the Jewish People.

There are several reasons WHY Satan is so focused on the destruction of Israel and the Jewish People.

א **G-d loves the Jews and He loves Israel**. In Torah, G-d says concerning Israel, *"For you are a holy – set apart – people to the LORD your G-d: the LORD your G-d has chosen you to be a people for Himself, a special treasure above all the peoples on the face of the earth."* [Deuteronomy 7:6]

"The LORD did not set his love upon you, nor choose you, because you were more in number than any people; for you were the fewest of all people: But because the LORD loved you, and because he would keep the oath which he had sworn unto your fathers, (Abraham, Isaac and Jacob) has the LORD brought you out with a mighty hand, and redeemed you out of the house of bondmen, from the hand of Pharaoh king of Egypt." [Deuteronomy 7:7]

ב **It was through the Jewish people that G-d inspired and gave the world the Holy Bible:** the Tanakh (Jewish Old Covenant) and the Brit Chadashah.(Jewish New Covenant). [The *Book of Luke* in the New Covenant may have been written by a Gentile but we do not know for sure.]

ג **It was through the seed line of the Jewish people from which Mashiach was born.** Both Yosef's and Miryam's family tree trace back to King David. <u>Yosef (the husband of Miryam) has his family line going back to Solomon, son of King David.</u>

See Brit Chadashah, the *Book of Mattiyahu* (*Matthew*) Chapter One, verses 1-17.]

Miryam—*the virgin-maiden who conceived miraculously by the Ruach HaKodesh*—has her seed line on her father's side going back to Nathan, son of King David. [See the *Book of Luke*, Chapter Three, verses 23-31.]

Miryam's family tree was recorded—as was Jewish custom—on the men's side of the family, so it started with Yosef's father-in-law, Eli.

Editor's Note: See Verse 23, *"Yeshua was about thirty years old when he began his public ministry. **It was supposed** that he was a son of Yosef who was of Eli."*

At any time, anyone who opposed Yeshua—*concerning him being the Messiah*—could have gone to the Temple (similar to local courthouse records today) and proven Him false if He were. **That was one thing of which the religious leaders NEVER accused Yeshua. His credentials were EXACT: Messiah, Son of David.**

T It was the Mashiach of Israel who HEALED the separation between G-d and man as a result of Adam's fall" in the Garden of Eden. The eternal BLOOD of the Everlasting Covenant paid for the sins of a fallen human race. The Lamb of G-d–Mashiach–took our sins upon Him [*as Isaiah the Prophet foretold 700 years before*] and ... **"by His stripes we are healed."**

*"But he was wounded for **our** transgressions, he was bruised for **our** iniquities: the chastisement of **our** peace was upon him; and with his stripes we are healed."*

*"In fact, it was **our** diseases he bore, **our** pains from which he suffered; yet we regarded him as punished, stricken and afflicted by G-d. But he was wounded because of **our** crimes, crushed because of **our** sins;* ***the disciplining that makes us whole fell on him,*** *and* ***by his bruises [stripes] we are healed."*** [Tanakh: Isaiah 53:4-5]

His blood was holy. He was perfect G-d and perfect man. Born of a virgin—**through a miracle of the Ruach HaKodesh (the Holy Spirit)**—His blood did not contain sin from an earthly father in Adam's'seed line. Yeshua came from the Father G-d. To this Man **the ancient Rabbis testify.**[51] This blood from the Lamb of G-d, **poured out for me and for you,** is sufficient atonement—payment and covering—for our souls. [Torah: Leviticus 17:11]

ח Messiah will NOT come [return again] **until Israel acknowledges Him and invites Him—pleads with Him—to come and bring deliverance. Then, the Deliverer will come to Zion. It is very plain ... If Satan can wipe out the Jews and Israel, the Mashiach can NOT return!**

*"I will go and return to my place, till they acknowledge their offence, and seek my face: in their affliction **they will seek me earnestly.**"* [Tanakh: Hosea 5:15]

The "affliction" spoken of will be the **Time of Jacob's'Trouble.** *"Alas! For that day is great, so that none is like it: it is even the time of Ya'akov's' [Jacob's'] trouble; but he shall be saved out of it."* [Tanakh: Jeremiah   30:7]

This will be last half (42 months) during the Seven Year Covenant that Israel will make with the Palestinians. At the very end of the seven years Mashiach will return **when the Jewish people invite Him—*plead with Him*—to return**. Those last three and one-half years (42 months) of the Seven Year Peace Treaty **will be worse than the Nazi Holocaust …** especially for those Jews living in *Ezor Yehuda VeShomron—Judea and Samaria area, or West Bank.*

I When Messiah comes—as King—He will destroy the enemies of Israel and set up His earthly Kingdom, ruling from Jerusalem. He will deliver His people.

"In that day the LORD will defend the inhabitants of Jerusalem … It shall be in that day that I will seek to destroy all the nations that come against Jerusalem." [Tanakh: Zechariah 12:8-9]

104

"I will destroy the strength of the goyim kingdoms."
[Tanakh: Haggai 2:22]

"And I will pour upon the house of David, and upon the inhabitants of Jerusalem, the spirit of grace and of supplications: and **they shall look upon me whom they have pierced***, and they shall mourn for him, as one mourns for his only son, and shall be in bitterness for him, as one that is in bitterness for his firstborn."*
[Tanakh: Zechariah 12:10]

And one will say to him, *"What are these wounds between your hands?"* Then he will answer. *"Those with which I was wounded in the house of my friends."*
[Zechariah 14:4]

"In that day there shall be a fountain opened to the house of David and to the inhabitants of Jerusalem for sin and for uncleanness." [Zechariah 13:1]

So now you know **WHY** Satan hates the Jews and Israel:

א G-d loves the Jews and He loves Israel.

ב It was through the Jewish people that G-d inspired and gave the world the Holy Bible.

ג It was through the seed line of the Jewish people from which Mashiach was born.

105

ד It was the Mashiach of Israel who HEALED the separation between G-d and man as a result of Adam's' fall in the Garden of Eden.

ה Messiah will NOT appear—He will not return again—until Israel acknowledges Him and invites Him—*pleads with Him*—to come and bring deliverance. Then, the Deliverer will come to Zion. **If Satan can wipe out the Jews and Israel, the Mashiach can NOT return!**

ו When Messiah comes – as King – He will destroy the enemies of Israel and set up His earthly Kingdom, ruling from Jerusalem.

Now you know WHY the Jews—and Israel—have suffered and been opposed so much throughout history. And now you know WHY the Jews are back in Eretz Israel after nearly 2,000 years of dispersion. It is time **soon** for Mashiach to come to Israel and set up His Messianic Kingdom. But—before He returns—the worst Holocaust[39] the Jews have ever experienced will happen: the Prophet Jeremiah called it the **Time of Jacob's'Trouble**.

What you are seeing and hearing in the news is the "sign" of the preparation of Israel for a great spiritual awakening in which multitudes of Jews turn to Mashiach Yeshua during the worst Holocaust[52] the Jews have ever known.

Let's back up. At what times in history—and WHY— were the Jewish people attacked in a manner as to wipe out the whole Jewish race? Let me name three:

▪ In Egypt, under Pharaoh, all the Hebrew male children were ordered to be killed at birth

▪ In Judea, under Rome, all the Hebrew male children from two years old and under were ordered to be killed.

▪ In World War II, under Nazi Hitler, six million Jews were murdered.

Over 7 million Christians were killed, also, between 1933 and 1938. However, **most were probably only Christians in name**. While they killed Jews simply for being Jews, it is probable that most of the so-called "Christians" were NOT killed for simply being a Christian.

Christians by name or religious affiliation, were killed usually for being Polish or subversive—or, because they were the Italians, French, Poles, Dutch, Austrians, et al who were fighting to stop Hitler long before the US even decided to get involved.

NOTE: My friend, Rachmiel Frydland, was able to sneak in and out of the Warsaw Ghetto and preach to his Jewish brethren about Messiah Yeshua the night before

107

many were killed by the Nazis. Read his testimony: *How I Escaped from the Nazis*.[53]

The clandestine reason for the attacks against Jews in Egypt, Judea and World War II was to destroy the Jewish race so that Mashiach—the Messiah of Israel—would NOT come to deliver Israel and establish His Kingdom.

> ■ Had the slaughter of all the male children in Egypt succeeded, there would have been NO Moshe (Moses).

> ■ Had the slaughter of all the male children in Judea succeeded, there would have been NO Yeshua (Jesus).

Each of these first two attempts … at least ONE child—a "chosen" one—escaped.

If the enemy can wipe out the Jewish People, as was the goal in Nazi Germany, there will be NO second appearing of Messiah to Mount Zion.

> *"And I will pour upon the house of David, and upon the inhabitants of Jerusalem, the spirit of grace and of supplications: and **they shall look upon me whom they have pierced**, and they shall mourn for him, **as one mourns for his only***

son, and shall be in bitterness for him, as one that is in bitterness for his first born."

– Tanakh: Zechariah 12:10

For the Messiah to appear the second time, the Jewish People have to be in their land—which they are now—and recognize Him as the One Who was pierced and by whose stripes they have been made whole. (Tanakh: Isaiah Chapter 53)

As stated previously, Messiah will NOT appear—return again—until Israel acknowledges Him and invites Him— *pleads with Him*—to come and bring deliverance. Then, the Deliverer will come to Zion. It is very plain … **If Satan can wipe out the Jews and Israel, the Mashiach can NOT return!**

"I will go and return to my place, till they acknowledge their offence, and seek my face: in their affliction they will seek me earnestly." – Tanakh: Hosea 5:15

The Hebrew Scriptures inform us that **in the End Times two-thirds of the Jewish People will be killed: worse than the Holocaust under Nazi Germany**. Only 33 percent of the Jewish People will remain.

"And it shall come to pass, that in all the land, says the LORD, two parts therein shall be cut off and die; but the third shall be left therein." –Zechariah 13:8

The Holy Bible also tells us, *"And it shall come to pass in that day, that I will seek to destroy all the nations that come against Jerusalem."* – Zechariah 12:9

So now we know the major energy of the Mystery Matrix—the Who, the Why and the What—of resistance and opposition to the Jewish People and Israel for past centuries up to the present. **But how does this apply to non-Jews, the Gentiles? And … how does it apply to the future.** Remember, God's blessings on humanity have issued forth from Abraham and Israel. Even non-Jews are—and will be—affected by what happens to Israel.

Satan hates both Jews and Gentiles … but he knows that the blessings of God for the whole human race were programmed to evolve from and through the Jewish People and Israel: they are God's Chosen People.

There will be a more subtle approach by Satan—and it is already being carried out—through the agency of DNA corruption, GRIN technology and "other worldly" players. **It is being devised not only to deceive Jews but Gentiles, also.**

Part of the construct by Satan in these beginning days of the End Times is a repeat performance. We will discuss this later in the book along with some **specific revelations concerning the Mystery Matrix.** But for now, let's look at some NEW signs.

NEW SIGNS

Let's look at some NEW signs that are actually OLD signs. Messiah Jesus said:

*"And **as it came to pass in the days of Noah**, even so shall it be also in the days of the Son of man. They ate, they drank, they married, they were given in marriage, until the day that Noah entered the ark, <u>and the flood came, and destroyed them all</u>.*

*Likewise even **as it came to pass in the days of Lot**, they ate, they drank, they bought, they sold, they planted, they built; but <u>in the day that Lot went out from Sodom it rained fire and brimstone</u> from heaven, and destroyed them all. After the same manner shall it be in the day that the Son of man is revealed."* – Luke 17:26-30

If you study both Torah contexts closely that Jesus referred to—**Genesis Chapter 6 for Noah … and Genesis Chapter 19 for Lot**—even a casual perusal gives evidence that great wickedness was present on the earth.

In Genesis 6:5 we read, *"And the LORD saw that the wickedness of man was great in the earth, and that every imagination of the thoughts of his heart was only evil continually."*

In Genesis Chapter 19 we see that God judges Sodom because of the prevalence of homosexuality being practiced there. When the two angels from God came to Lot's house to deliver him and his family, we read:

"But before they lay down, the men of the city, [even] the men of Sodom, compassed the house around, both young and old, all the people from every quarter; and they called unto Lot, and said unto him, ***Where are the men that came in to you tonight? Bring them out unto us, that we may know them.***

And Lot went out unto them to the door, and shut the door after him. And he said, I pray you, my brethren, do not so wickedly. Behold now, ***I have two daughters that have not known man; let me, I pray you, bring them out unto you, and do ye to them as is good in your eyes****: only unto these men do nothing, forasmuch as they are come under the shadow of my roof."*

The homosexuals in the city wanted to practice perversity on the two men (the angels) who were Lot's guests. This was deemed such wickedness by Lot that he was willing even to let the men abuse his own daughters in exchange for the safety of the men (the angels).

So we see that in both contexts there was **great wickedness—which will also be prevalent upon the earth in the End Times**. We know this from the *Book of*

Revelation, also. **However, there is something extra concerning the "Days of Noah."**

"And it came to pass, when men began to multiply on the face of the ground, and daughters were born unto them, that the **sons of God** <u>saw the daughters of men</u> *that they were fair; and they took them wives of all that they chose.*

And Jehovah said, My spirit shall not strive with man for ever, for that he also is flesh: yet shall his days be a hundred and twenty years.

The Nephilim were in the earth in those days, <u>and also after that</u>, when the sons of God came unto the daughters of men, and they bear children to them: *the same were the mighty men that were of old, the men of renown.*

And Jehovah saw that the wickedness of man was great in the earth, and that every imagination of the thoughts of his heart was only evil continually." – Genesis 6:1-5

This brings to question: **Who were the Nephilim?** And, who were the "**sons of God**" spoken of in context here? In the Book of Job, verse 6, we read: *"Now it came to pass on the day when the* **sons of God** *came to present themselves before Jehovah, it was that Satan also came among them."*

The Hebrew phrase for "sons of God" and "bnai Elohim — בני אלוהים" is used three times and **always refers to "angelic host"** but does NOT differentiate between holy angels or fallen angels. **It does NOT refer to humans as "children or sons of God.**

Also, in Genesis 6:12 we read, *"And God saw the earth, and, behold, it was corrupt; for all flesh had corrupted their way upon the earth."* But, Noah was a righteous man with a wife and three sons and their three wives, who found favor in the eyes of the LORD.

Evidently the seed line—the DNA—of the human race had become so corrupt that God had to destroy the whole earth, except for Noah and his family. Possibly Noah's faith—anointed by Ruach HaKodesh (the Holy Spirit) —protected him from corruption of his DNA.

Since we know that good—or holy—angels would NOT have been involved in the seduction or sexual intercourse with "the daughters of men," it would have been "fallen angels." In the *Book of Jude* we see more light on this.

*"And the **angels which kept not their first estate, but left their own habitation**, he has <u>reserved in everlasting chains under darkness unto the judgment of the great day</u>.*

*Even as **Sodom and Gomorrha**, and the cities about them in like manner, **giving themselves over to*** *fornication, and going after strange flesh*, are set forth for an example, <u>suffering the vengeance of eternal fire.</u>" (Jude verses 6 and 7)

First we see references to both signs of the End Times which Messiah Jesus talked about: **the days of Noah ... and the days of Lot**. However, notice that Jude mentions "*angels which kept not their first estate, but left their own habitation.*" Another translation would be, "*the angels that did not keep within their original authority, but abandoned their proper sphere ...*"—or—"*the angels who did not keep their proper domain, but left their own abode.*"

It is this author's opinion that *The Living Bible* has an accurate paraphrase of Jude:1-4:

> "*Now a population explosion took place upon the earth. It was at this time that **beings from the spirit world looked upon the beautiful earth women and took any they desired** to be their wives. Then Jehovah said, "My Spirit must not forever be disgraced in man, wholly evil as he is. I will give him 120 years to mend his ways.*"
>
> ***In those days, and <u>even afterwards</u>, when the evil beings from the spirit world were sexually involved with human women, their children became giants***, *of whom so many legends are told.*" – TLB [30]

115

These giants were the Nephilim. **When Joshua went into the Promised Land he and the Israelites encountered the Rephaim and Nephilim**. Remember, David killed Goliath, a giant of nine feet in height.

Here is another thing—although NOT scripture—that is worth considering:

Every prominent ancient culture has stories of beings—*usually referred to in some manner*—as gods who interfaced with humans; that is, part human–part angel. As discussed previously, we have a divine record in the Scriptures and they were designated as *sons of God—b'nai Elohim.*

Other ancient textual writings, such as the *Book of Enoch*, relate the belief of a mixed race of part human–part angel beings referred to as "Watchers." several almost complete copies of *the Book of Enoch* in Aramaic were found among the Dead Sea Scrolls, and it is clear that whoever collected the scrolls considered it a vitally important text.

Even more intriguing is the fact that additional, previously unknown or little-known texts about Enoch were discovered at Qumran among the findings with the Dead Sea Scrolls. The most important of these is *The Book of Giants*.[31]

However, it is the opinion of this author that *The Book of Giants* is NOT a trustworthy source as many scholars consider the older sections—mainly in *The Book of the Watchers*—to **date from about 300 BCE**. Conversely, there are those who give credence to the *Book of Enoch*, as we shall next discuss.[32]

The *Book of Enoch* was still in existence centuries before the birth of Christ. It was considered scripture by many early Christians. The earliest literature of the so-called "Church Fathers" was filled with references to it. It's interesting that the Second and Third Century "Church Fathers"—Justin Martyr, Irenaeus, Origin and Clement of Alexandria—all quoted from the *Book of Enoch*.

Tertullian (160-230 CE) referred to the *Book of Enoch* as "Holy Scripture." **The Ethiopic Church even added the *Book of Enoch* to its official canon. It was widely known and read the first three centuries after Christ.** However, it became—along with many other books—discredited after the Council of Laodicea. Thereafter it was not disseminated until around the time of the Protestant Reformation.

Then, there was a revived interest in the *Book of Enoch*. By the late 15th Century rumors began to spread that somewhere a copy of the long lost *Book of Enoch* might still exist. During this time many books arose claiming to be the long-lost book and were later found to be forgeries.

The return of the long lost *Book of Enoch* to the modern western world is credited to the famous explorer James Bruce, **who in 1773 returned from six years in Abyssinia with three Ethiopic copies of the lost Book of Enoch.**[33] [34]

So now, let me ask you a question: Are the Nephilim:

> **Still here?**

> **Coming back?**

So just as in GRIN technology and synthetic biology, we see external players—other worldly beings—altering gene lines—DNA—of the human race.

WHY? The answer is the same NOW as it was THEN:

- To destroy the Messianic bloodline.

  - Originally to keep Messiah from being born.

  - In the End Times, to stop Messiah's return.

- To "hatch" a breed of rebels.

  - People who will be subservient to Satan.

  - Candidates for 10 Regional Leaders.

EXTERNAL PLAYERS

Over ten years ago at the University of Excellence we discussed four (4) areas of Boolean commonality that were trending as follows:

- False Messiah Trends and Signs

- Family Fidelity

- Fallen Spirits

- False Treaties

I don't need to share the statistics with you that today HALF of Christian marriages end in divorce. But let me share something with you that should wake you up!

POSTULATE #1: Two (2) of the four (4) sectors of Boolean commonality we discussed online at the *University of Excellence* were—or will be—directly related as we enter the End Times to family fidelity. Those two are as follows:

- Fallen Spirits; and,

- False Messiah trends and signs.

POSTULATE #2: At the time of the First Edition of this book, there was an "overlay" of highly positive correlation of linear regression to the following:

- Disruption of Nuclear Family Fidelity; and,

- Patterns of social underpinning attributed to the coming FALSE Messiah (the anti-Christ). We are NOT referring to the REAL Messiah who is to come!

EDITOR'S'NOTE

Before you judge this strictly objective study or any personal association to me as the writer-reporter, please note TWO things: **1.** I am NOT a Republican, Democrat or Libertarian. I have voted for all three of these parties in the past; **2.** Two of the last three Presidents of the USA since 2009 have demonstrated (because of their policies) anti-Israel leanings.

There are patterned socialization characteristics of the above-mentioned two postulates. But for now, let's continue with both analyses and prophecies concerning the External Players.

FAMILY FIDELITY

Let me speak prophetically. A great dichotomy of offensives will soon start to happen in the FAMILY structure. **At the same time the true family structure of man and woman is being eroded by same sex marriage, there will be a revitalization of holy family structures**: a revival … a spiritual bonding … a godly melting together of the REAL family. Many previously divorced couples will re-unite in marriage. Many family and inter-personal relationships will be healed.

There will **be the ministry of Eliyahu (Elijah) the prophet** that will "turn the hearts of the fathers to the children and the hearts of the children to their fathers." – Tanakh: Malachi 4:5-6

FALLEN SPIRITS

There will be satanic combinations: "demonic doubles" working increasingly in the end-times.

Demonic Double #1 – Islam and politically oriented Leftist-Socialists. These will work unwittingly with Islam for a while … until which time the Islamic Caliphate starts attacking them, also. **Why do Ivy League leftists support—and in some cases—work with Hamas, ISIS and Islamists? Because these elements hate Jews, real Christians, Israel AND the USA foundations based upon Judeo-Christian heritage.** They are demonically inspired —and possessed at times like ISIS—to fulfill an End Time objective for Satan.

Demonic Double #2 – False Religion and Demons. These will establish strongholds in the United Nations, WEF, media and independent governmental entities and work from within to then attack outwardly against Israel, the Jews and real Christians.

Here's a "sleeper" for you to watch: **Germany**. Just as under Nazi control during World War II, many people did NOT speak up against the political attacks against real Christians and Jews—especially the Jews—this type of attack will increase. WHY? **The same regional strongholds of "religion" and "demons"—when working in combination—become synergistic in their offensives.**

The same demon spirits that operated in Nazi Germany are still ALIVE today. Demons do NOT die. They are disembodied spirits that seek to inhabit live bodies: human or animal.

MY PROPHECY

A dichotomy of spiritual offensives will evolve:

- One—**godly**—will arise with powerful prophetic anointings from the same geographic areas that have been anti-Jewish and anti-Israel. Even from areas like Middle East Islamic entities, including ISIS and terrorist organizations: **Miracle agents!**

- The other—**demonic**—will be end-time works orchestrated for use by the Global FALSE mashiach (anti-Christ) to suppress Jews and **real** Christians in the end-time.

It is possible that fallen spirits may begin to inter-breed with humans while—*at the same time*—through use of genome altering implants on "willing" subjects prepare a **"submissive leadership core"** for the anti-Christ as he implements his system of political, economic and military control on Planet Earth. This may include the **Ten Regional Leaders** who are appointed by the Global Governance Leader (FALSE mashiach) anti-Christ to help govern the nations. These "willing subjects" MAY be from a DOUBLE source:

■ Politically expedient recipients of the "**Mark of the Beast: his mark, or his name, or the number of his name**." Those who will take the "mark" so they can buy or sell or carry on commerce; and those who did not want to be beheaded for not taking the mark. (See Brit Chadashah: Revelation Chapter 13.)

■ Some feel these will be **willing** subjects of alien abduction who receive genome altering implants. **There are other more scripturally based options as to HOW people may receive the genome altering implants or hybridization**; however, alien abduction of humans for the purpose of genome alteration should not be ruled out as a possibility.

However, let us digress here and discuss the subject of **alien abduction of humans** in the next section of this book.

UFO'S AND ALIEN ABDUCTIONS

Since April, 2013, there have been between 900 and 1,000 UFO's reported monthly. Deception is the name of the game in the End Times. According to the Book of Revelation, men will NOT repent of their lies, fornications, stealing, idolatry and murders. So, **deception will be the "hallmark" of the part of society** NOT marked by the Spirit of God. **However, I am referring here to another area of deception**. That which is imposed upon "willing" human subjects. By "willing," I am talking about those who do NOT filter or judge messages by the G-d's Word and Spirit of God.

There has been much research conducted and many books written—with valid investigations—concerning alien abduction. Researchers and authors such as Honorable Paul Hellyer,[48] L. A. Marzulli,[46-B] Dave Stinnett, Jim Wilhelmsen, Gary Stearman, Stan Deyo, Major George Filer[47] (US Air Force Retired), Stephen Bassett, Dr. Roger Lier,[45,46-A] Chris Putnam and many others.

The mysterious world of UFOs has captured the imagination of people for decades. In recent years, the U.S. government has shown a renewed interest in unidentified aerial phenomena (UAP), leading to the creation of the Advanced Aerial and Anomalous Research Organization (AARO). Now, a series of whistleblowers have come forward, shedding light on covert reverse engineering programs happening right under our noses in Washington D.C.

Unveiling the Enigma: **Whistleblowers Reveal Covert UFO Reverse Engineering Programs in Washington D.C.**

The mysterious world of UFOs has captured the imagination of people for decades. In recent years, the U.S. government has shown a renewed interest in unidentified aerial phenomena (UAP), leading to the creation of the Advanced Aerial and Anomalous Research Organization (AARO). Now, a series of whistleblowers have come forward, shedding light on covert reverse engineering programs happening right under our noses in Washington D.C. In this exclusive exposé, we delve into the astonishing claims made by these insiders.

The AARO Task Force

The bipartisan UAP legislation passed in USA in late 2022 marked a significant step in addressing the UFO phenomenon. The task force's primary objective is to investigate and understand UAPs and their potential implications on national security. Notably, **the legislation also explicitly acknowledges the existence of UFO crash material, indicating a growing willingness to investigate such incidents.**[102]

- NASA must take an active role and decide to fund proposals directly on the UAP subject.

- Congress must mandate funding via, for example, the National Science Foundation, to support research on UAP.

- AARO to be more open, within understandable constraints of classification, to releasing their case investigations, and especially, of course, the case investigations for sightings which they cannot resolve. [113]

- The American Security Drone Act of 2023 (which is integrated into the **2024 National Defense Authorization Act**) already prevents federal agencies from using drones from countries deemed national security threats. That measure hints at a broader trend toward banning or severely limiting the use of Chinese drones in the U.S.

Alien abductions and implanted objects have been verified. **One thing to note is that aliens lie to humans with such falsehoods as:**

- We created you;

- We want to **enhance** you; and,

- We want to deliver you from your life chaos.

Alien life-forms are many times tangible:

- They show up on multiple radars simultaneously;

- They leave radioactive traces and evidence like burnt grounds;

- They are NOT bound by physical laws:

  - ➤ They make 90 degree turns at super high speeds.

  - ➤ They fly faster than the speed of sound with no sonic boom.

Dr. David Jenkins has conducted over 1,000 hypnotic regressions of people claiming to be alien abductees. In addition, Dr. Roger Leir [46-A] has conducted the removal of implants supposedly placed by aliens during abductions. **Common scenarios of abduction are as follows:**

- Abductions are at night when subjects sleep;

- The subjects are taken aboard a UFO;

- The subjects clothes are removed; and;

- The subjects receive a medical procedure.

There have been NO abductions by aliens of people who refused OR used the name of Jesus (Yeshua) to resist.

So, **let's get back on track and discuss more scripturally based options** as to HOW people **may** receive genome altering implants or hybridization. (You might want to watch *Shadow Government and Alien Abductions* at YouTube or Odysee.)

Much research is being carried out today in areas of development of a "hybrid" species: i.e., harvesting of human fetuses. **Remember, there was gene pool corruption in Noah's'day** which resulted in God destroying the whole earth by the Great Flood; only eight (8) righteous souls were left: Noah, his wife, his three sons and their wives. **The "sons of God" took wives of those whom they chose.** *Notice: as we discussed previously, the "sons of God" **never** refers to "believers" in the Tanakh, the Hebrew Scriptures.*

1 Peter 3:19-20, 2 Peter 2:4-5 and Jude 6 refer to the fallen angels who procreated with the daughters of man in the Days of Noah (before the Flood). This resulted in the **"Nephilim:" "the fallen ones"** … or … **"ones who cause others to fall."** We know from scripture that the "fallen angels" who took to themselves the "daughters of men" (associated time wise with the Days of Noah and the Great Flood) have been bound in everlasting chains for their just judgment of everlasting fire.

However, **the offspring of the "fallen angels"**—the Nephilim—were drowned in the Great Flood. That is, **their bodies drowned**; however, their spirits could be

129

the demons we read about in the Brit Chadashah (the New Testament). **Demons never die!**

Plus, we know *"there were giants on the earth in those days (the days of Noah), and also afterward ..."* – Torah: Genesis 6:4. And, in the conquest of the Promised Land—and up into the time of Kind David.

The development of a hybrid species in the end times – **through which the "Beast"—anti-Christ—MAY derive his submissive leadership core**—could well be the result of fallen spirit forces (demons) facilitating the same, **rather than aliens from another planet**. These fallen spirit forces (demons) may be from extra-dimensional time-space: **not from other planets**, but from a megaverse (outside our traditional concept of space-time continuum).

OPTION C: TEN REGIONAL END-TIME LEADERS

Could some of the powerful executives of MNC's (Multi National Corporations) provide the "work source" for the "10 Kings" referred to ten times in the Holy Bible?

In Tanakh, Book of Daniel, we read, *"He ... will greatly honor those who acknowledge him. He will make them rulers over people and will distribute the land at a price."* (Daniel 11:39, NIV.) This is from a portion of Daniel's prophetic description of the implementations of the New Global Governance Leader—the FALSE mashiach (anti-Christ).

Daniel prophesies that "elites" of some status will receive mega rewards for their support of this end-time incarnate spirit of Satan. Specific KEY people who acknowledge him and accept his authority will receive a reward of land. **"Land" in its Aramaic form used here would also include "economic domain, property or geographic area."**

These "elites" are bought off for their loyalty … and made rulers over many!

FALSE TREATIES: These are treaties designed by Satan to prepare the way for the reception of his agent: the false messiah (anti-Christ). These are treaties based upon "wind." They have NO substance. They are—or may be—easily broken … and have no practical or pragmatic "teeth." One typical example is the agreement between USA, Russia and Syria (Obama and Putin) concerning the destruction of chemical weapons.

Another clear example is the nuclear talks with Iran in 2015. Even during those talks North Korea supplied several shipments of missile components to Iran and the transfers appeared to violate United Nations sanctions on both countries, according to U.S. intelligence officials.

Just as a side note, **I told Israel in August, 2008,** NOT to be deceived by (then) current peace talks by Olmert and Assad. At that time Obama and USA wanted to force Israel into negotiations with Damascus.[41] I warned Israel

131

NOT to do it. Listen to (or read show notes) of my podcast: *Israel, New Forces in Middle East Parlance.*[36]

False treaties will increasingly be made between sharply contradicting nations, cultures, philosophies and national interest groups. The major mission of the *University of Excellence* is to utilize Boolean logic to analyze such happenings in current geopolitical processes.

You will see more of these false treaties as we enter more deeply into the End Times. Deception is a major symptom of the anti-Christ anointing, and will manifest itself in the Seven Year Treaty between Israel and the Palestinians when it is initiated. **It will be the biggest mistake Israel ever makes!**

The mainstream populace of the world is uneducated as regards geopolitical processes. Read this *"1912 Junior High Exam"*[37] from the state of Kentucky, USA. Is it any wonder the Chinese are economically overtaking the USA and Europe?

FALSE MESSIAH: I believe the "false messiah" (anti-Christ) is alive today. I also believe he is operating in governmental and political circles today. **I believe he does NOT yet know exactly his role as governed by Satan. I believe he has NOT yet been incarnated by Satan.** However, I believe he willingly deceives the populace over whom he governs, as well as other nations and has—even at this time—the goal of "world leader." This goal will finally morph into the goal of "world domination" as his body becomes overtaken and incarnated by Satan.

The "false messiah" will claim to solve the world's problems including war, energy, religious differences, poverty and sickness PLUS:

- Heal the Israeli-Arab land dispute; and,

- Allow the Jews to build their temple in Jerusalem on the Temple Mount.

When the coming world leader—*appointed by the New Global Governance*—takes over, he will make a treaty (a covenant) with Israel for seven years. Today, in addition to disease and famine issues, the leaders of the dominant nations are concerned with three (3) primary factors:

- Attaining peace among nations and ethnic groups;

- Guaranteeing the flow of oil; and,

- Stopping terrorism and conflict in the Middle East (especially between Israel and the Palestinians).

And the chief bargaining factor will be the city of Jerusalem.

Remember, the **false** messiah (the anti-Christ) will make a seven year treaty with Israel,[38] and **in the middle of the seven years he will break the treaty**, go into the Jewish Temple (which he will allow to be built on the Temple Mount in Jerusalem as part of the stipulations of the treaty) and desecrate it by declaring that he is god. This will begin the worst Holocaust[39] the Jewish People and Israel have ever experienced.

SUMMARY: There are four F's that are important for Israel—and for YOU—to watch:

- Family Fidelity

- Fallen Spirits

- False Treaties

- False Messiah trends and signs

These four F's will help you discern the times more accurately **IF you do pattern matching** [40] in conjunction with Demonic Doubles #1 and #2 described above. I am NOT talking about pattern recognition; I am talking about pattern matching: I am talking about exact algorithmic origins: source replication of malevolent intent but with different outward shells.

The Four F's and the Demonic Doubles are just highly observable strings in everyday life and current news. Let's use **pattern recognition**[41] to see if we can observe all the string carriers associated with the payload. I postulate that by doing this, we will observe **the Mystery Matrix**, which we will now discuss on the following pages.

THE MYSTERY MATRIX

In reference to the tribes of Planet Earth, two **predominant aggressors** have actuated throughout the history of Planet Earth:

▪ Destruction of the Jewish People and Israel.

▪ Corruption of the Human DNA.

EDITOR'S NOTE

It is my opinion that any change of the basic structure of the DNA should be considered **corruption** of the DNA as placed into being originally by the Creator. For example—*as discussed previously*—researchers at the University of Copenhagen are worked on a **third strand of DNA**—a synthetic hybrid of protein and DNA—a tri-strand, which would be **"synthesizing life that is utterly *alien* to this world"** [and help them] "to put together a novel combination of molecules that can self-organize, metabolize, grow, reproduce and evolve."[24]

In a span of time as young as Planet Earth—*as we have recordation*—the above two actuations have occurred at various times and places. Let's talk about the predominant aggressors:

⬤ DESTRUCTION OF JEWS AND ISRAEL

The goal was FIRST to disallow Messiah from coming to Planet Earth—since He would be born through Jewish seed line—to redeem mankind through the agency of His sacrifice on the cross-stake at Jerusalem.

The goal NOW is to disallow Messiah from returning to Planet Earth—since the Jews will have to invite Him back—to setup His Kingdom and rule from Jerusalem.

⬤ CORRUPTION OF THE HUMAN DNA

Based on information we have already covered, we observe that the primary mission of the Mystery Matrix is a conflation of the following **goals concerning YOU**:

- Being tempted to sacrifice your autonomy.

- Being "setup" to lose your children's DNA.

- Being handed over to the Global Citizenry.

- Being hindered from knowing Messiah.

- Being blocked from forever living in Heaven.

Now, let's observe the string players—the carriers of the payload—in the Mystery Matrix. We have already identified by design goals the following ten players:

- Genome modification

- Robotics

- Information technology (AI)

- Nanotechnology

- Cognitive science

- Technological singularity

- Synthetic biology

- Geopolitics and 10 regional leaders

- Global guides

- External players

Most of the above group (inclusive of GRIN and NBIC)—other than the last three—are NOT inherently evil, if utilized with restraint and with guidelines based upon morality and ethics. But when the **profit motive or the desire for unbridled power and control** overrides these there is danger. But, this is true of any human endeavor: from conception, through research and development, and into production and marketing.

However, we must also consider the gridlines that encompass **the whole panorama of human enhancement**. It is NOT the humans that are involved with the development of any of the above—no matter how evil they may be. *This is NO excuse for the motives or actions of immoral or evil people.* When we look at the whole picture as filtered through the lens of Holy Scripture it is easy to see that **Satan—that old serpent, the devil—is the one who is orchestrating the plans**.

The Mystery Matrix is designed to utilize any or all of the above 10 carriers to facilitate various objectives. There is *at this time* a hidden geopolitical "behind–the-scenes" amalgamation—a spiritual collusion—both human and other-worldly that is being orchestrated to facilitate **control …** of YOU and your family and of the world.

We are at the threshold of **the most cataclysmic—the worst and most evil—change in society** that Planet Earth has ever known.

This change is at the same time malevolent **and** opaque to most of society. I'm NOT talking just about the New World Global Governance—although that's part of it. I'm talking about what we have discussed in this book so far: **something so sinister—and at the same time—so appealing to every thinking person**.

139

I'm talking about something that has its "core association" in age-old Biblical history: **the interaction of fallen spirits with humans on earth**. Plus—*at this moment*—on the cutting edge of science and technology: **corruption of the human DNA**. Both serve the same purpose for Satan, regardless of the motives or reasons of the player-carriers—be they fallen angels or humans involved in research and development.

Don't be mistaken! Even though the triad of **government, military and education is spending millions of dollars in R & D**—with the financial support of banks and corporations—there is an unseen, dark force behind the "push" forward.

Don't worry about being left behind at the appearing of Messiah—that is, IF you KNOW Him. What you need to worry about NOW is you and your children being either **betrayed OR being left behind**—*in competition*—**by enhanced humans with more cognition and ability than you**.

Remember—singularity and time are working against you—unless you are operating in the will of God.

Will enhanced-humans automatically receive the *Mark of the Beast*?

Let's review HOW robotics can and may be used to serve the **New Global Governance**[22]. Here are some ways in which robotics may serve the Evil Empire:

■ Image of the Beast

■ Monitoring public places and individual houses and businesses (robots would be assigned to specific addresses with legal warrants).

■ Security – NOT your security, but the government's.

■ Housing "shell" for AI of the Anti-Christ demonic system to carry out orders. i.e., Robots may be used to perform orders programmed into them via Artificial Intelligence (AI).

The purpose of AI is to posture—copy and transfer—human thinking into non-human systems.

Through nanotechnology and the use of "vectors" bio-scientists now have a new method of transferring—transporting—sub-atomic material.

The "vectors" are essentially biological "trucks" that transport DNA building materials AND agents—*workers*—into human cell structure.

Nanotechnology can be—and is already being— used to produce changes *inside* the host's body. Nanotechnology potentially provides the ability to order and change molecular and atomic structures. The same basic building blocks are present in humans as are in the natural world, thus enabling nanotechnology to change human tissues and cells at the molecular level.

Remember, one nanometer is **one-billionth** of a meter.

A "vector" can be any vehicle that can carry—transport—genetic information and gain entry into a cell. And ... with genetic mapping ... **once inside the cell, the "workers" go about their respective jobs** of:

■ Splicing human genes at predetermined locations; **or,**

■ Filing genetic information that can be—at any time—downloaded for production of NEW—hybrid—cells.

WARNING: These cells are NOT just "enhanced" cells. **They will no longer be human.**

Even If new hybrid cells are not produced, the very fact of **enhancement**—due to the influence of uncertainty, let's call it what it is: modification—**could easily have deleterious results. Here are just a few examples**:

■ Brain modification allowing receptors to gain access to—or receive messages from—sources that are either paranormal or occult and Satanic.

■ Downloading—via the transfer of artificial intelligence (AI) information—through brain-machine interfacing, a desire for the "Mark of the Beast."

■ Corrupted spermatozoa which could fertilize an ovum producing a hybrid being: a non—*other than normal*—human life form.

■ Receiving fallen—demonically anointed—influence via psycho-neural pathways.

Automatic control systems—*especially as regards to Artificial Intelligence (AI) via input to the human brain*—that implement Brain Machine Interfacing (BMI) and Nanotechnology will result in **internal programming that will substitute for Normal Human Nature ...** which is concomitant with Transhumanism (= beyond human).

We discussed how through **technological singularity** events may become unpredictable, unfavorable, or even unfathomable. And, we quoted Elon Musk, PayPal and Tesla electric car genius, who stated that, "with artificial intelligence, we are summoning the demon," and placing **AI as more of a potential threat to the annihilation to the human race than nuclear war**

In 2010 there was a new type of life placed in artificial genetic material and chemically synthesized into cells that grew. The life form was given the name Synthia.

143

The question is—morally, ethically, medically and scientifically—**can we now originate life forms by reverse engineering**: from digital code to DNA and living cells? If so, **what is the NEW definition of "human?"** And, with neither soul nor hope, what—*and who*—dictates their future?

Let me suggest that you reflect on the statements of two well known individuals. One speaks as a prophet; the other one is a Prophet.

> ■ Genetic engineering, robotics, "AI" artificial intelligence and nanotechnology—present *"a different threat than the technologies that have come before. Specifically, robots, engineered organisms, and nanobots share a dangerous amplifying factor. They can self-replicate. A bomb is blown up only once—but one bot can become many, and quickly get out of control."*
>
> – Bill Joy, Co-Founder of Sun Microsystems
>
> ■ *"But you, O Daniel, shut up the words, and seal the book, even to the time of the end: many shall run to and fro, and* **knowledge shall be increased.***"*
>
> – Daniel the Prophet / Tanakh: Daniel 12:4

NEW DANGERS OF AI:
CONTINUE ADVANCED RESEARCH?

An artificial intelligence expert with more than two decades of experience studying AI safety said an open letter calling for a six-month moratorium on developing powerful AI systems does not go far enough.

Eliezer Yudkowsky, a decision theorist at the Machine Intelligence Research Institute, wrote in a recent op-ed that the **six-month "pause" in developing "AI" systems more powerful than GPT-4"** called for by Tesla CEO Elon Musk and hundreds of other innovators and experts understates the **"seriousness of the situation."** We would go further, implementing a moratorium on new large AI learning models that is "indefinite and worldwide."

NOTE: The six month pause is probably NOT going to happen----*now or in the future*--because the "Big Boys" (Google, Facebook / Meta, etc.) are NOT supporting it.

The letter, issued by the Future of Life Institute and signed by more than 1,000 people, including Musk and Apple co-founder Steve Wozniak, argued that **safety protocols need to be developed by independent overseers** to guide the future of AI systems.

"Powerful AI systems should be developed only once we are confident that their effects will be positive and their risks will be manageable," the letter said. Yudkowsky believes this is insufficient.

For Yudkowsky, the problem is that an AI more intelligent than human beings might disobey its creators and would not care for human life. Do not think "Terminator." *"Visualize an entire alien civilization, thinking at millions of times human speeds, initially confined to computers in a world of creatures that are, from its perspective, very stupid and very slow,"* he writes.

Yudkowsky warns that *"there is no proposed plan for dealing with a superintelligence that decides the most optimal solution to whatever problem it is tasked with solving is annihilating all life on Earth."* He also raises concerns that **AI researchers do not actually know if learning models have become "self-aware" and whether it is ethical to own them if they are.**

Stargate and DeepSeek are the two new arrivals on the scene. Stargate's goal is to build massive AI infrastructure. **Beware of future "AI Agents" if you value you privacy and future!** Study this yourself.

China's **DeepSeek** (probably built from AI stolen from USA) can ultimately be the weapon of dictators and terrorists! Finally, be very concerned about the development of AGI and ASI. The only thing we MAY devise is to have "layers of control" for protection.

Prince Handley recommends Elon Musk's xAI. xAI is a company working on building AI to accelerate human scientific discovery.

146

ISRAEL, ISIS AND INFORMATION

Boolean analysis tells us that currently there are **three major trends** peaking with acceleration:

- Israel

- ISIS (reorganization of the Caliphate)

- Information (AI) technology

Which one do you vote for?

Both GRIN and NBIC interface with information technology and specifically with artificial intelligence (AI). Lots of research is being done behind closed doors but with the enhancement of funding by governments and corporations. Add to this the **open source availability on the internet of formulae and instructions on HOW to make deadly viruses capable of mass destruction that can be utilized by terrorists.**

GRIN and NBIC are both emerging technologies. NBIC is more advancing in the Cognitive Science area, but both technologies are basically the same in core development. They do NOT require large warehouses or manufacturing plants—*or resources*—to create or develop implements of mass destruction. PLUS there is the ability for multiplicative reproduction.

Of the three current major trending areas noted above, we know from Scripture that **Israel is the only one that wins**. But, HOW does this apply to us—*and to our children*—in the very near future?

One of our purposes in writing this book was **to help YOU be able to detect the *Mystery Matrix* as it is evolving NOW ... and in the future!**

Remember, the two **predominant aggressors** that have actuated throughout the history of Planet Earth are:

- Destruction of the Jewish People and Israel.

- Corruption of the Human DNA.

Terrorist organizations like ISIS **all** hate the Jews and Israel—and **real** Christians. This is a basic premise of their teachings from the Qur'an. Satan hates the Jews and Israel—and **real** Christians.

As for the "corruption" of human DNA, it will serve the same Satanic purpose whether it comes about from Nephilim modalities or from laboratory research.

The **combined** strategy of Satan is to keep Messiah from returning to Planet Earth and to keep YOU—*and your children*—from knowing the Messiah personally and being able to live in Heaven forever.

Wars will happen we know. The anti-Christ will show up we know. The False Prophet will arise we know. But what we do NOT know is **HOW God will use us** to delay, hinder and war against the forces of Evil.

That's **another reason for writing this book**. I know from the Holy Bible that hard times are coming. However, **I do NOT have to let them come upon me or my children**. I can—*and do*—delay and hinder the dark works of Satan, and WAR against the forces of Evil.

I have found a SECRET. **The secret is through prophetic decrees—*through creative prophecy*—as given by revelation of the Holy Spirit**. You and I as intercessors—**operating in prophetic ministry**—can make specific prophetic decrees in the Name of Yeshua the Messiah—against evil empires, evil research and development, and evil forces such as terrorist groups..

We can also decree prophetically the salvation of individuals and groups involved in malevolent ventures. And, we can decree prophetically—**in the Name of Yeshua the Messiah**—frustration, confusion and failure into the camps, laboratories, legislation and funding of ungodly people and activities.

If you are Jewish and find it uncomfortable to pray in the name of Yeshua (Jesus), then decree prophetically in the Name of HaShem. The LORD God will know Who it is!

And remember to PRAY for Israel and for the peace of Jerusalem. All who do so will prosper. (Psalm 122:6)

Watch and pray … that you may be counted worthy to stand before the Son of Man (Yeshua) and to escape the things that are coming upon the earth. Above all, if you do NOT know the Messiah, PRAY and ask Him into your life as your LORD; ask Him to direct you and fill you with the Holy Spirit.

Pray this prayer:

> *"God of Abraham, Isaac and Jacob, if Yeshua (Jesus) is really my Messiah, reveal Him to me and I will serve you. Amen!"*

"Call to me and I will answer you and show you great and mighty things which you do not know."
— Tanakh: Jeremiah 33:3

LIVE A LIFE OF EXCELLENCE!

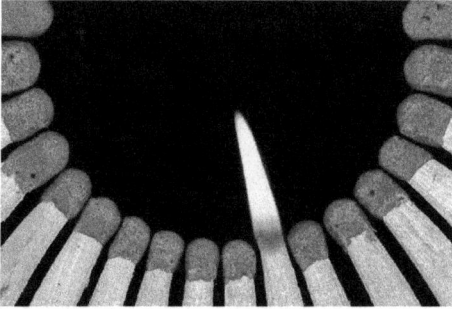

If you want to know specifically what will happen in the next decade—and in the remaining days of Planet Earth— you need to study the following companion books in the *Prophecy Series* by Prince Handley:

Map of the End Times

Flow Chart of Revelation

Prophecy, Transition & Miracles

Babylon the Bitch – Enemy of Israel

Prophetic Calendar of Israel and the Nations

OTHER BOOKS BY PRINCE HANDLEY

LISTED ON TWO PAGES

- Map of the End Times
- How to Do Great Works
- Flow Chart of Revelation
- Action Keys for Success
- Health and Healing Complete Guide to Wholeness
- Prophetic Calendar for Israel & the Nations: Thru 2023
- Healing Deliverance
- How to Receive God's Power with Gifts of the Spirit
- Healing for Mental and Physical Abuse
- Victory Over Opposition and Resistance
- Healing of Emotional Wounds
- How to Be Healed and Live in Divine Health
- Healing from Fear, Shame and Anger
- How to Receive Healing and Bring Healing to Others
- New Global Strategy: Enabling Missions
- The Art of Christian Warfare
- Success Cycles and Secrets
- New Testament Bible Studies (A Study Manual)
- Babylon the Bitch – Enemy of Israel

- Resurrection Multiplication – Miracle Production

- Faith and Quantum Physics – Your Future

- Conflict Healing – Relational Health

- Decision Making 101 – Know for Sure

- Total Person Toolbox

- Prophecy, Transition & Miracles

- Enhanced Humans – Mystery Matrix

- Israel and Middle East – Past Present Future

- Anarchy and Revolution: A Prophecy

- Real Miracles for Normal People

- Sexual Immorality: Addiction of Loss

- Healing Toolbox Plus: A to Z Workshop

- Anointed Strategies: Power Plays

NOTE: Many Prince Handley books are available on Audible.

PLUS … DON'T MISS PRINCE HANDLEY
99 CENT "FAST READ" MINI-BOOKS
"SPIRITUAL GROWTH SERIES" [114]

AVAILABLE AT AMAZON AND OTHER BOOK STORES

UNIVERSITY OF EXCELLENCE PRESS
San Diego ▪ London ▪ Tel Aviv

Go to following pages for BONUS materials

&

Bibliography

BONUS

To help you, and to help you teach others, we have prepared **Rabbinical Studies** at this site:

https://www.uofe.org/biblical-studies.html
(Scroll down)

These are commentaries from **ancient** Jewish Rabbis that identify the Mashiach of Israel.

To help you, and to help you teach others, we have also prepared **Bible Studies** in English, Spanish and French.

- **English** FREE Bible Studies
  www.uofe.org/biblical-studies.html

- **Spanish** FREE Bible Studies
  www.uofe.org/biblical-studies.html

- **French** FREE Bible Studies
  www.uofe.org/biblical-studies.html

BIBLIOGRAPHY

1.Wired Magazine, *"Why the future doesn't need us."* November 14, 2005.

http://archive.wired.com/wired/archive/8.04/joy_pr.html

2. USA: NSF/DOC sponsored report. 2003, *Converging Technologies for Improving Human Performance*, Kluwer Academic Publishers (currently Springer). The Netherlands.

3. Eden, Amnon; Moor, James; Søraker, Johnny; Steinhart, Eric, eds. (2013). *Singularity Hypotheses: A Scientific and Philosophical Assessment*. Springer. p. 1.

4. Carvalko, Joseph (2012). *The Techno-human Shell-A Jump in the Evolutionary Gap*. Sunbury Press. ISBN 978-1620061657.

5. Kurzwell, Ray. March 7, 2001. *The Law of Accelerating Returns.* http://www.kurzweilai.net/the-law-of-accelerating-returns

6. Wadhwa, Vivek. April 24, 2015. *The Coming Problem of Our iPhones Becoming More Intelligent Than Us.* Singularity HUB. Published by Singularity University.

http://singularityhub.com/2015/04/24/the-coming-problem-of-our-iphones-being-more-intelligent-than-us/

7. May 12, 2015. *One step closer to artificial intelligence: Scientists create cells replicating human brain processes.* RT News. http://rt.com/news/257993-artificial-intelligence-scientists-brain/

8. February 26, 2015. *First head transplant possible within two years, says Italian 'Frankensurgeon.'* RT News. http://rt.com/news/235843-canavero-head-transplant-surgery/

9. Science Clarified_com. http://www.scienceclarified.com/Ga-He/Genetic-Engineering.html

10. http://en.wikipedia.org/wiki/Robotics

11. Harris, Tom. How Robots Work. *"Robots and Artificial Intelligence."* How Stuff Works. http://science.howstuffworks.com/robot6.htm

12. Minsky, Marvin. *The Emotion Machine.* Simon & Schuster; First Edition edition (November 7, 2006).

13. Nelson, Brian. April 25, 2013. MNN. "Mother Nature Network. *7 real-life human cyborgs.*" http://www.mnn.com/leaderboard/stories/7-real-life-human-cyborgs

14. Cornish, Edward *"The 1990s and Beyond,"* World Future Society, 1990.

15. Pearson, Ian. 1998, 2000.

16. *An Asimov-Style Question for 2014: What Will Life Be Like in 2064?* Radio Free Europe / Radio Liberty. January 3, 2014.

17. Simmons, Dan (1996). *Hyperion Cantos.*

18. National Nanotechnology Initiative. www.nano.gov

19. *Texas Engineers Build World's smallest, Fastest Nanomotor.* http://www.popularmechanics.com/science/health/a10657/worlds-tiniest-motor-is-500-times-smaller-than-a-grain-of-salt-16811274/

20. Istvan, Zoltan. March 10, 2014. *A New Generation of Transhumanists Is Emerging.*

21. *Robotic Surgery*, www.childrens.com. Children's Health[sm.]

22. *New Global Governance*. University of Excellence. http://uofe.org/new_global_governance.html

23. *First Self-Replicating Synthetic Bacterial Cell*. J. Craig Venter Institute. jcvi.org/cms/research/projects

24. Scientific American, Dec. 2008, *Triple Helix: Designing a New Molecule in Life*. Peter E. Nielsen.

25. Programs – Competition. iGEM 2015. *Synthetic Biology based on standard parts*" http://igem.org

26. Smithsonian. *Total Recall*. Natural Sciences: Steve Ramirez and Xu Liu, Noonan, David. November, 2014.

27. Knopf. *Nothing to be Frightened Of*, September 2, 2008. http://www.dailyvillain.com/project/?tag=grin-technologies Barnesm Julian.

28. *The Living Bible*. Tyndale House. 1974. ISBN:10 0842322477; ISBN 13: 9780842322478.

29. Heller, Jacob and Peterson, Christine. *Human Enhancement and Nanotechnology*. Foresight Institute.

30. *The Living Bible*. Tyndale House Publishers, Inc. (October 18, 1974)

31. Dead Seas Scrolls Texts. "*The Book of Giants.*" The Gnostic Society Library.

32. McCracken, Andy. "*The Book of Enoch. A Modern Translation of the Ethiopian Book of Enoch.*"

33. "*An Ethiopian Journal.* The Book of Enoch". https://tseday.wordpress.com/2008/09/14/the-book-of-enoch/

34. Video. *"The Book of Enoch,"* documentary made by History Channel: Banned From the Bible - –he History Channel (parts 5/6); In Ethiopia.

35. 2012, January 23rd· "*German anti-Semitism deeply rooted in society*". BBC. With analysis by Stephen Evans, BBC News / Berlin.

http://www.bbc.com/news/world-europe-16678772

36. Handley, Prince. "*Israel: New forces In Middle East Parlance.*" http://podcastsatellite.libsyn.com/israel-new-forces-in-middle-east-parlance July 15, 2009

37. *"1912 Eighth Grade Examination."* Bullitt County,

Kentucky, USA.
http://www.bullittcountyhistory.com/bchistory/schoolexam1912.html

38. Podcast Satellite, *"Bibi, Babylon and 'Bama: Land for Peace, Petra and Prophecy."*
http://podcastsatellite.libsyn.com/bibi-babylon-and-bama-land-for-peace-petra-and-prophecy,
June 18, 2009, Prince Handley

39. University of Excellence. Blog & Podcast: *"How to Recognize the FALSE Mashiach (NOT the REAL one)."'*

https://podcastsatellite.libsyn.com/how-to-recognize-the-false-mashiach. January 3, 2023

40 Wikipedia. *"Pattern matching."*
http://en.wikipedia.org/wiki/Pattern_matching

41. Pattern recognition. *Images.*
https://www.google.com/search?q=pattern+recognition&tbm=isch&tbo=u&source=univ&sa=X&ei=IKExVZS9G8myogTyoYGgDw&ved=0CH8QsAQ&biw=1025&bih=458

42. *"Obama insists that Israel ..." Israel and the Middle East."* University of Excellence.

http://www.uofe.org/israel_and_middle_east.html#Oba
ma_insists_that_Jerusalem_&_Israel_be_divided

43. *Inheritance: Logic Gates.* College of Engineering -
Department of Computer Science. Virginia Tech. Spring
2008. CS2605 - –ab 8.
http://courses.cs.vt.edu/~cs2605/spring08/Labs/8/Lab0
8.pdf

44. Fox News / Armed Forces. *"Scientists in Poland
working on liquid body armor."* April 15, 2015.

45. Walia, Arjun. April 19, 2014. *"Alien Implants: A
Closer Look Into One Aspect of Alien Abduction."* CE:
Collective Evolution.
http://www.collective-evolution.com/2014/04/19/alien-
implants-a-closer-look-into-one-aspect-of-alien-
abudction/

46. Jacobs, David M., Ph.D. International Center for
Abduction Research. www.ufoabduction.com/index.htm

46-A Leir, Dr. Roger. *Turkey UFO clearly shows aliens.*
http://www.alienscalpel.com/updates/turkey-ufo-clearly-
shows-aliens-dr-roger-leir

46-B Marzulli, L.A. (Author and Researcher). *Politics,*

Prophecy and the Supernatural. The Watchers Series. Nephilim. Alien abductions.

47. *"E.T. Shot at Ft. Dix."* Filer, George F., Major US Air Force Intelligence. UFO sightings.
https://www.youtube.com/watch?v=F87FjkqLol4

48. *Extraterrestrial Issues.* Re: Hellyer, Paul (Honorable). http://en.wikipedia.org/wiki/Paul_Hellyer

49. *Israel: A Plain Path.* Handley, Prince. March 1, 2009. Podcast Satellite

http://podcastsatellite.libsyn.com/israel-a-plain-path

50. *Confidential Intel for Israel.* Handley, Prince. February 9, 2009. Podcast Satellite.

http://www.podcastsatellite.libsyn.com/index.php?post_id=432594

51. *The Ancient Rabbis testify of the identity of Mashiach (Messiah).* University of Excellence.

http://www.uofe.org/RABBINICAL_STUDIES.html

52. BLOG: *The Preparation of Born-Again Israel.* (The worst Holocaust is coming.) University of Excellence.

http://www.uofe.org/princehandley__blog_.html#BLOG:
_World_News_Prep_Born_Again_Israel

53. Frydland, Rachmiel. *How I Escaped from the Nazis.*
http://www.faithandreasonforum.com/index.asp?Pagel
D=37&ArticleID=108

54. *"How artificial intelligence could be violating our human rights."* LIFE > Tech. October 8, 2018. Independent.co.uk

55. Pulak Satish Kumar. Your Story. *"Top three predictions for humanoid robots in 2019."* December 20, 2018.

56. Allison Barrie. *"June Beetles Conscripted Into Cyborg Army."* FOX News Firepower. March 24, 2016.

57. Weisberger, Mindy. *"Bug-Sized Robot Competitors to Swarm DARPA's 'Robot Olympics.'"* Live Science. July 21, 2018.

58. Samuels, David. *"Is Big Tech Merging with Big Brother?"* Wired Magazine. January 23, 2019.

59. Wang, Yudoesn't*"China Is Quickly Embracing Facial*

Recognition Tech, For Better and Worse." Forbes. July 11, 2017.

60. *"What are possible dangers of nanotechnology?"* https://www.wisegeek.com/what-are-the-possible-dangers-of-nanotechnology.htm

61. *"Nanotechnology Risks."* FutureforAll.org. (Future Technologies and Their Effect on Society.) https://www.futureforall.org/nanotechnology/risks.htm

62. Cuthbertson, Anthony. *"Elon Musk says Neuralink Machine that Connects Human Brain to Computers 'Coming Soon.'"* The Independent | News. April 22, 2019.

63. Tucker, Patrick. *"The Newest AI-Enabled Weapon: 'Deep-Faking' Photos of the Earth."* www.nextgov.com April 1, 2019.

64. University of Copenhagen. *"Scientists create new technology and solve a key puzzle for cellular memory."* www.phys.org August 16, 2018.

65. SYNTHEGO. *"CRISPR Cuts"* Podcast. www.synthego.com/podcast June 11, 2019.

66. *"Introducing the CRISPR Gene Knockout Kit – Version 2."* www.synthego.com June 12, 2019.

67. Bosley, Catherine. | Bloomberg. *"Robots on track to wipe out a tenth of manufacturing jobs by 2030: Report."* www.Business-Standard.com. June 26, 2019.

68. Evans, Martin. [Crime Correspondent]. *"Artificial Intelligence tool used to catch people who lie to the police."* www.telegraph.co.uk. January 7, 2019.

69. Etherington, Darrell. *"Elon Musk's Neuralink looks to begin outfitting human brains with faster input and output starting next year."* www.techcrunch.com. 16 July, 2019.

70. University of Leeds. "ScienceDaily. *"A rrobotic revolution for urban nature."* January 4, 2021

www.sciencedaily.com/releases/2021/01/210104 131938.htm

71. Kemp, Richard. *"Trends in information technology law: looking ahead to 2021."* Kemp IT Law. 5 January 2021. https://www.kempitlaw.com/trends-in-information-technology-law-looking-ahead-to-2021/

72. Colaner, Seth. *"Agility Robotics' humanoid Digit robot helps itself to the logistics market."* 12 November 2020.

73. *"Micro-Robots in Your Veins."* Midnight Call. Lexington, SC USA. January 2021.

74. Roy, Sujoy. *"AI Singularity, where are we heading?"* CARRE4. 6 November 2020

75. *"Doubling lifespan with in vivo based editing of genetic disease."* BioTechScope. 7 January 2021. https://doi.org/10.1038/s41586-020-03086-7

76. Brown, Tim and Rommelfanger, Karen. *"The Social Impact of Brain Machine Interfaces: Value Sensitive Design in Neurotechnology."* The Euroethics Blog. Emory University Center for Ethics. 15 September 2020.

77. Britt, Hugo. *"Elon Musk's 'Great and Terrifying' Brain-Machine Interface: Neuralink."* https://www.thomasnet.com/insights/elon-musk-s-great-and-terrifying-brain-machine-interface-neuralink/ 25 August 2020.

78. Fan, Shelly. *"Meet Assembloids: Mini Human Brains with Muscles Attached."* Singularity Hub, Singularity University. https://singularityhub.com/2021/01/12/meet-assembloids-mini-human-brains-with-muscles-attached/ 12 January 2021.

79. bowmo™, Headquarters, 99 Wall Street, Suite 891 New York, NY 10005, AI based HR Recruiting for Recruiters, Employers and Applicants. https://bowmo.com/services/

80. Chris Pandolfo and Matt Finn: Fox News. *"Leaders call for temporary halt of artificial intelligence development."* https://www.foxnews.com/tech/ai-expert-warns-elon-musk-signed-letter-dodoesn'tnough-literally-everyone-earth-will-die March 30, 2023.

81. *Julia Musto: Fox News. "UN agency calls on governments to implement global ethical framework for AI."* https://www.foxnews.com/tech/un-agency-calls-on-governments-implement-global-ethical-framework-ai March 30, 2023

82. By Staff at Glenn Beck, February 9, 2023 https://www.iheart.com/content/2023-02-09-glenn-beck-blog-is-your-job-safe-here-are-5-unlikely-

industries-that-could-be-replaced-by-ai/

83. By Fionna Agomuoh, digital trends. *"ChatGPT: How to use the AI chatbot everyone's talking about."* March 30, 2023.

84. OpenAI *"So what is ChatGTP?"* https://openai.com/blog/chatgpt. November 30, 2022.

85. *"What is ChatGPT?"* https://chat-gpt.org/

86. *Sharon Goldman.* VentureBeat [VB Daily] *"The hidden danger of ChatGPT and generative AI"* https://venturebeat.com/ai/the-hidden-danger-of-chatgpt-and-generative-ai-the-ai-beat/ December 5, 2022.

87. Connie Loizos, TechCrunch [TC]. *"Is ChatGPT a 'virus that has been released into the wild'?"* https://techcrunch.com/2022/12/09/is-chatgpt-a-virus-that-has-been-released-into-the-wild/ December 9, 2022.

88. Science Daily. [from Cell Press*]. "What should we call evolution driven by genetic engineering? Genetic welding, says researcher."*

https://www.sciencedaily.com/releases/2023/03/23032
8145225.htm. March 28, 2023.

89. Grace Browne. Wired [cites CGS' 'atie Hasson] / 03-17-2023. *"It's Official: No More Crispr Babies—for Now."* https://www.geneticsandsociety.org/article/its-official-no-more-crispr-babies-now

90. Adam Zewe, MIT News Office. *"Robotic hand can identify objects with just one grasp."* https://news.mit.edu/2023/robotic-hand-can-identify-objects-just-one-grasp-0403. April 3, 2023.

91. Ashley Watters, *"Emerging Trends in Information Technology for 2023."* https://connect.comptia.org/blog/emerging-trends-in-information-technology. March 17, 2023.

92. Emma Colton. Fox News TECH. *"AI could go 'T'rminator,' 'ain upper hand over humans in Darwinian rules of evolution, report warns."*

https://www.foxnews.com/tech/ai-could-go-terminator-gain-upper-hand-over-humans-in-darwinian-rules-of-evolution-expert-warns April 4, 2023.

93. Dan Hendrycks. Center for AI Safety. *"Natural Selection Favors AIs over Humans."*

https://drive.google.com/file/d/1p4ZAuEYHL_21tqstJO
GsMiG4xaRBtVcj/view [pdf] April 3, 2023.

94. Pohang University of Science & Technology
(POSTECH). ScienceDaily. *"R"volutionary battery
technology to boost EV range 10-fold or more."*
"www.sciencedaily.com/releases/2023/03/2303290918
06.htm. March 29, 2023.

95. Lacey Christ. Fox News Trending. "Rep.
Lance Gooden calls Artificial Intelligence 'v'ry
scary,' 'rges action 'b'fore it's'too late"…"
https://www.foxnews.com/politics/te171yriaongres
sman-lance-gooden-warns-very-scary-
consequences-ai-overcomes-american-society.
April 5, 2023.

96. Michael Nolan. IEEE Spectrum. *"Neuralink's FDA
Troubles Are Just the Beginning."*
https://spectrum.ieee.org/neuralink-seeks-fda-approval
April 2, 2023.

97. Emily Mullin. WIRED [Science]. *"All the Actually
Important Stuff Neuralink Just Announced."*
https://www.wired.com/story/all-the-actually-important-
stuff-neuralink-just-announced/ December 1, 2022.

98. Prince Handley *"Israel's Future Wealth."*

https://podcastsatellite.libsyn.com/israels-future-wealth. September 25, 2018. (Tishri 15, 5779)

99.. Alexander Ward, Matt Berg, Lawrence Ukenye. Politico | National Security Daily. *"Why Iran is helping Russia against Ukraine."*

https://www.politico.com/newsletters/national-security-daily/2022/10/21/why-iran-is-helping-russia-against-ukraine-00062898. October 21, 2022.

100. Haley Britzky, CNN. *"Top US general says increased partnership between Iran, Russia, and China will make them 'problematic' for 'years to come.'"* *https://www.cnn.com/2023/03/29/politics/china-russia-iran-us-mark-milley-nuclear/index.html.* March 31, 2023.

101. Baris Balci and Selcan Hacaoglu. Bloomberg [Politics]. *"Turkey Seeks to Be First NATO Member to Join China-Led SCO."*

https://www.bloomberg.com/news/articles/2022-09-17/turkey-seeks-china-led-bloc-membership-in-threat-to-nato-allies?leadSource=uverify%20wall. September 18, 2022.

102. LUFOS. *"Whistleblowers Reveal Covert UFO Reverse Engineering Programs in Washington D.C."* https://www.latest-ufo-sightings.net/2023/04/unveiling-the-enigma-whistleblowers-reveal-covert-ufo-reverse-

engineering-programs-in-washington-d-c.html. April 6, 2023.

103. Reuters, *"Tesla's Musk predicts AI will be smarter than the smartest human next year".* April 8, 2024.

104. DeepMind CEO Demis Hassabis Explains What Has to Happen to Achieve AGI, Business Insider. *Business Insider* October 19, 2024.

105. "If Ray Kurzweil Is Right (Again), You'll Meet His Immortal Soul in the Cloud". *Wired.* June 13, 2024.

106. Science News / Johns Hopkins University, *"Robot that watched surgery videos performs with skill of human doctor, researchers report,"* November 11, 2024

107. Podcast Satellite, *"Israel: Daniel Warned You About the Ten Kings"* January 17, 2024, Prince Handley

https://podcastsatellite.libsyn.com/israel-daniel-warned-you-about-the-ten-kings

108. AP News: *"How it Happened: Two Seismic Weeks,"* December 8, 2024, Jill Lawless

109. Times of Israel, *"PM: Israel wants 'correct' ties with new Syrian regime, but will attack if necessary,"* December 11, 2024, Lazar Berman and TOI Staff.

110. Stanford University, School of Humanities and Sciences, *Study finds ChatGPT's latest bot behaves like humans, only better,* February 22, 2024, Cameron Scott.

111. New York Times | Health Systems, *AI Chatbots Defeated Doctors at Diagnosing Illness,* November 22, 2024.

112. PC Gamer | News, *"Elon Musk says his brainchip patients will soon 'outperform a pro gamer','then takes a big old puff and says 'let's give people superpowers'.'* August 5, 2024, Rich Stanton.

113. Space Insider, *Understanding UFOs: What has to happen in 2025 to move the UAP story forward? December 30, 2024,* Leonard David.

114. Fast Read 99 Cent Mini-Books *"Spiritual Growth"* https://www.amazon.com/s?k=Spiritual+Growth+books +by+Prince+Handley

ANNOUNCEMENT

We recommend you obtain the companion books to this book. *Map of the End Times* discusses in detail the End Time events that will take place on Planet Earth. The eBook *Flow Chart of Revelation* is full of links and resources and focuses on the "judgments" that will be unleashed on Planet Earth during the end times. It is an easy-to-follow **time-line** of the events described in The Book of Revelation. And, *Babylon the Bitch: Enemy of Israel* reveals HOW the enemy of Israel will try to juxtaposition Babylon (a real future city) in opposition to Jerusalem, both spiritually and physically. Geopolitical and secret intel is included.

Plus, to know **HOW to WAR successfully** against GRIN, NBIC and "external players" of the End Times—*all that's involved in the Mystery Matrix*—you need the book: *Prophecy, Transition & Miracles*.

✝

UNIVERSITY OF EXCELLENCE PRESS
San Diego ■ London ■ Tel Aviv

www.ingramcontent.com/pod-product-compliance
Lightning Source LLC
Chambersburg PA
CBHW061721020426
42331CB00006B/1031